8/16

P9-DNW-252

DISCARDED

9   I want! I want!

Pub. by W Blake 17 May 1793

When we were young

two centuries of children's book illustration

WILLIAM FEAVER

HOLT, RINEHART AND WINSTON · NEW YORK

To Jane, Emily, Jessica and Silas

HALF TITLE
William Blake
'I want! I want!', engraving from
For Children: The Gates of Paradise,
London 1793

FRONTISPIECE
Anonymous
Page from a scrapbook,
c. 1885

CONTENTS PAGE
W. Heath Robinson
Vignette from *The Incredible Adventures of Profesor Branestawm,*
London 1933

Y 741.64
1979

The illustration from IN THE NIGHT KITCHEN by Maurice Sendak
(Copyright © 1970 by Maurice Sendak) reprinted by permission
of Harper & Row, Publishers, Inc.

Library of Congress Cataloging in Publication Data

Feaver, William.
    When we were young.

    1. Children's books, Illustrated. 2. Illustration of books.
I. Title.
NC965.F42   741.64'2   76-29901

ISBN Hardbound: 0-03-020306-6
ISBN Paperback: 0-03-020301-5

Designed and produced by Thames and Hudson, London

Printed and bound in the Netherlands

Contents

Two centuries of children's book illustration

A CHILD SETS FOOT on a ladder to the moon. 'I want! I want!' it cries, pleads, demands. But, as we all know, innocence lapses into experience. The ladder will fall.

The image of impending disillusion comes from William Blake's *For Children: The Gates of Paradise*. It was published in 1793. Round about then a real child, bored no doubt with the stream of questions – 'What distance is the moon from the earth?' 'How many moons has Jupiter?' – in his *An Easy Introduction to Geography*, drew his seedy, ill-shaven, evil-eyed tutor on the flyleaf. Ideally, I suppose, children should illustrate their own books. Illustration must have originated in doodles.

The wag poking fun and Blake conjuring up his vision, the one childish, the other sublimely childlike, are extremes; most illustrations for children are less spontaneous or ambitious. They are designed to make books more attractive, impressive, sales-appealing. All the same, the best ones have always conveyed hints of conspiracy, between author and illustrator and between illustrator and child. With nostalgia as a guideline, the artist steals back into childhood and shares what he remembers.

'Childhood is the nearest to true life,' André Breton said in his first Surrealist manifesto. Over the past two hundred years childhood has come to represent more than pre-puberty. It's seen as a state of readiness, a state of mind open to exploitation. Sentimentalists regard 'the tender years' as a constant, idyllic bygone. In their view childhood imagery should charm, all Greenaway dimples and daisy chains; no fears, no growing pains. 'How wide the Gulf and Unpassable between Simplicity and Insipidity,' Blake remarked. Like Rousseau shortly before, he saw childhood as a phase of freedom ending, almost unavoidably, in betrayal, in 'mind-forg'd manacles' and in crying for the moon. 'There is no use in education. I hold it wrong. It is the great Sin.' It follows that the only defence for innocents against the powers that be are fantasy, parody, mockery: Surrealist weapons and childish responses.

Accordingly in illustration everything is shown to be possible. In picture-form metaphors blossom. Princes turn into toads (23). Animals act like humans (26, 32). Plants shoot up into the clouds. Giants roam and bluster like rogue adults (13) and shadows solidify or flutter like silhouette demons. No need to take the storyteller's word for it; there, on the page, the illustrator shows what happens. Through ridicule and exaggeration (two ways of expressing fears) he serves as intermediary and exorcist. In the end, the prince is restored to his human form and birthright. The bean-stalk is chopped down; the bully giant crashes to the ground and the shadows melt.

Childhood is a stage when it is still permissible to stare and demand instant explanations for everything, and so some illustrations have to be instructive as well as interpretative, providing cross-sections and bird's-eye views (79, 97, 101): Hows and

6

Child's drawing of his teacher on the flyleaf of
An Easy Introduction to Geography,
London 1807

Whys as distinct from irresponsible flights of fancy. Bishop Comenius, whose *Orbis Sensualium Pictus* of 1657 was probably the first purpose-made children's picturebook, believed that 'pictures are the most intelligible form of learning that children can look upon'. Increasingly, from the late seventeenth century onwards, children were provided with books of their own: primers, textbooks, storybooks. Sometimes entertainment competed with instruction. More often than not the two went together, overlapping and intertwining. Thus the questions and answers of *An Easy Introduction to Geography* were stilted schoolroom variants on church catechisms, unrelieved by illustrations; *Cobwebs to Catch Flies* (2) and other chapbooks were a little more attractive, being laced with engravings to set the scenes for each dialogue. But these too were riddled with sanctions. Dickens, who did so much to foster the mid-Victorian cult of childhood, often complained about the 'cool, impertinent inquiries' in the arithmetic books he had faced as a boy and the so-called story books that 'didactically improved all sorts of occasions from the consumption of a plate of cherries to the contemplation of a starlit night'.

At the burlesque end of the range, in catchpenny (i.e. second-hand woodblock) broadsheets, 'imageries' or 'Bilderbogen', and in 'nursery rhymes' (as they were categorized in the 1820s after centuries of use), the catechisms became rigmaroles and woodcuts headed every page.

As illustrative traditions lengthened, graphic imagery developed its own lines of descent. Tenniel's Alice (27, 28) is a direct descendant of the copperplate and woodcut heroines of the eighteenth century, Little Goody Two-Shoes and her like. She in turn inspired the Dorothy drawn by John Neill for L. Frank Baum's Oz books (51). These figures were given character as well as presence by the illustrators and served as links between wonderlands and normality. Places, whether topographic or fantastic, also developed in special ways. The super-colossal architecture of John Martin's Jerusalem (11) re-emerged in Little Nemo's Slumberland and Dan Dare's Interplanetary Space Fleet HQ.

Such interconnections and cross-currents are far from straightforward. Illustrators follow snakes-and-ladders courses. Sometimes, apparently, they leap years ahead of their time – in the inspired amateurism of Töpffer, for instance (12). More often they snake back into proven manners. Picture images and literary imagery may correspond well enough but a perfect match is hardly ever achieved except by an author-illustrator (Lear, Potter, de Brunhoff). And, of course, just as graphics veer away from their texts, no child's attention can be confined to books designed for its particular reading-age, so that for every 'children's classic' there are dozens of perennials that are impossible to classify. Many of the illustrations most enjoyed by children – Bewicks, Cruikshanks, Heath Robinsons – were not specifically intended for them. Equally, many of the collections of fairy stories illustrated by Dulac, Rackham and Nielsen are not children's books at all. They were produced as de luxe gift-objects for adults to browse through. *Perrault's Fairy Tales* and Galland's *Thousand and One Nights* were written for adults but soon passed into the juvenile category. Aesop became Uncle Remus (32).

When John Newbery started publishing his Juvenile Library in the 1750s he issued cut-down versions of *Robinson Crusoe* and *Gulliver's Travels* on a par with *Old Mother Hubbard* and *Little Goody Two-Shoes*. Illustrations eased the transition by emphasizing each key moment: the sight of Robinson Crusoe in his goatskins, of Aesop's fox snapping at the grapes, the Horse mocking the Ass, of Gulliver hauling the Blefuscan fleet. Children's books became a sanctuary for stories hitherto preserved by oral tradition (Robin Hood and Till Eulenspiegel) and throughout Europe publishers began to breed sub-species. Crusoe begat generations of castaways, notably *The Swiss Family Robinson*, first published in 1812. Fairies lay dormant for a while and then in the mid-nineteenth century swarmed everywhere. Bestsellers inspired imitations: Roscoe and Mulready's *The Butterfly's Ball* (4), for example, was such a hit in 1807 that rival attractions soon abounded: *The Peacock 'At Home', The Butterfly's Funeral, The Eagle's Masque, The Fishes' Feast, The Horse's Levée, The Elephant's Ball, the Fishes' Grand Gala, The Jackdaw's 'At Home', The Mermaid's 'At Home'*. So many follow-ups constitute a genre. The same happened with Hoffmann's *Struwwelpeter* (7, 9): sweetened and politicized variants became rife.

Children's book illustration is more than a publishing speciality. It is part of a wider popular culture. The leading figures, the fairy godmothers, the wicked uncles, the freaks, ogres, clowns and heroes parade as not so much literary creatures as a troupe of performers. Many of their exploits, outrages, role-reversals, comic turns, magical transformations and glittering finales entered books via theatre and sideshow. They took shape in the early nineteenth century, at the same time as the circus and pantomime were formulated in England and France, and in parallel terms. Death-defying acrobats climbed ladders to the moon, villains lurked with

daggers drawn, Puss in Boots proffered advice, Punch thumped Judy, the ringmaster
held sway. With a crack of the whip and a clearing of the throat to bring the audience
to order and the troupe to heel, with 'Once upon a Time', the story performances
began. The feats were recorded penny plain, tuppence coloured, on broadsheets, a
stream of ephemera that was to widen to include stickers and trade cards (54, 55),
cigarette cards (53) and pin-ups.

Children's book illustration is suspended in this welter of imagery, occasionally
bobbing into fine art waters but more often drifting in commercial shallows. A tiny
proportion survives to become classic. The fittest, not necessarily the most deserving.
Noddy and Superman remain, unaffected by condemnations of their characters and
appearance. Tenniel's portrayal of the Mad Hatter has outlived all others. Peter
Rabbit, Mickey Mouse and Babar seem imperishable. Hoffmann's 'Little Suck-a-
Thumb', 'Johnny Head-in-Air' and 'Struwwelpeter' have remained in print
continuously ever since they first appeared in 1845. Edward Lear's limerick
personalities have persisted since 1846 (10). Survival depends on continuing demand.
Ultimately children's tastes, not adult strictures, determine which shall be immortal.

But the point about the child crying for the moon is that it cannot know exactly
what it wants in advance. Both Hoffmann and Lear made their drawings for
particular children – Hoffmann's three-year-old son, Lord Derby's family – an ideal
situation. Inevitably, however, *Struwwelpeter* and *The Book of Nonsense* were inspired
and shaped to a great extent by the imagery their creators had been brought up on.
They are caricatured chapbooks. Blake's *Songs of Innocence and Experience* too are,
recognizably enough, based on chapbook formulae, relief-etchings substituted for the
usual artless woodcuts: neo-classicized a little, transfigured overall.

In this relay of imagery from childhood to childhood, themes snowball,
conventions proliferate. But each generation has to feed off what adults envisage,
publish and see fit to buy.

George Cruikshank
'The little tailors',
from *German Popular Stories*,
vol. 1, London 1823

George Cruikshank
'Peter Schlemihl sells his shado[w]'
from *Peter Schlemihl*,
London 1823–4

The history of children's book illustration is brief; little more than two hundred years if you discount its sporadic beginnings. But it is long enough to prove that, while the most extraordinary inventions, such as Lear's and Hoffmann's, have sprung from whims or, in the case of the Rev. Charles Dodgson (who did his own illustrations to the first version of *Alice*), out of 'a desperate attempt to strike out some new line in fairy lore', the dominant traditions – chapbook to picture book, to Crane toybooks, to Père Castor picture albums – developed well within the graphics industry and established children's book publishing. Indeed, most of the artists whose names have become synonymous with styles or modes – Greenaway, Caldecott, Heath Robinson – were all-purpose graphic artists who happened to hit on winning treatments of staple children's material: nursery rhymes, fairy stories. Success made them specialists.

In Newcastle upon Tyne, for example, Bewick illustration – both the method and the imagery – originated within the Beilby family glass and silver engraving firm where Thomas Bewick served out his apprenticeship doing graphic oddments. Setting himself up in business with his brother John, he took to making wood engravings of tickets, billheadings and decorative inserts – woodcut coats of arms, men-of-war, English monarchs, horses – for jobbing printers. Chapbook designs – ABCs, Little Red Riding Hoods, Robinson Crusoes – were added to his range. They were an obvious sort of stock in trade; an image bank which he then started using himself in his own publications, *A Pretty Book of Pictures for Little Masters and Misses*, *Tom Thumb's Playbook*, *The Life and Adventures of a Fly* and *Aesop's Fables* (6). Then, in his greatest, most ambitious works, *A General History of Quadrupeds* (1790) and *The History of British Birds* (1797 and 1804, 3), Bewick emerged from the near-anonymity of the workshop and became famous as an illustrator. The vignettes at the end of each chapter were a form of autobiography, scenes from Tyneside life, mainly as he remembered it years before: children scampering among gravestones, launching toy boats, molesting dogs, playing soldiers; adults fishing, journeying, peddling wares. Besides transcending previous images of childhood (the vignettes were, after all, more or less incidental to his natural history purpose), Bewick transformed wood engraving, and thus the art of illustration.

Using the end of the block instead of the side, thus working on the harder surface, against the grain, he coaxed half-tone effects, pinprick and hairline details, on to the box-wood, and so produced engravings robust enough to stand anything up to a million impressions before showing signs of wear.

In Bewick's hands and in the tradition he established, wood engraving was essentially a means of producing stilled, miniature images. Spontaneity was better expressed in lithography and, best of all, in etching, where the artist could scratch the plate as though drawing freehand and make every mark himself. The disadvantage of wood engraving was that very few illustrators could actually do it. Most of them had to make a drawing on the block and then hand it over to the engraver to do the best he could with it. Accordingly, the prudent artist made allowances to ease the translation. George Cruikshank, for one, so suited his style to what he knew his engravers could accomplish that there was often very little difference between his preliminary drawing and the published illustration.

Cruikshank was the most significant and influential illustrator of children's books from 1823, when he produced *German Popular Stories*, to the 1840s. In a career that lasted over seventy years – born in 1792, he died in 1878 at the height of the Crane and Greenaway era – he supplied illustrations for every age and need. When he was eight his father Isaac, a commercial artist with a bent for caricature, set him to work designing penny lottery sheets for children his own age. He soon progressed to etching broadsheet caricatures of every twist and turn in political and social life, using borrowed imagery most of the time, one idea needling the next. In the last years of the Regency, when caricature and public opinions ran riot, he illustrated squibs like *The Political House that Jack Built*, a parody chapbook, and it was only when the caricature market declined that he turned to books. In 1823 he illustrated *Peter Schlemihl*, the story of an innocent who sold his shadow to the Man in a Grey Coat: 'I saw him with a wonderful neatness take my shadow from head to foot . . . roll and fold it up neatly and at last pocket it.' The ominous predicaments and oddities in the tale only became apparent in Cruikshank's etchings: Peter Schlemihl cowering on a chair, watching the clock, everything but himself casting shadows, and, several escapades later, striding across Bering's Straits in Seven League Boots. Ninety years later Schlemihl was reborn, in more childish form, as Peter Pan. The same year and in much the same spirit Cruikshank illustrated *German Popular Stories*, the first English edition of the *Kinder und Haus Märchen*, 'collected by the Brothers Grimm from oral tradition' and originally published in 1812. 'Beauty, fun and fancy were united in these admirable designs,' Thackeray wrote in 1840. 'They have been copied all over Europe.'

Cruikshank showed the Golden Goose with a string of simpletons trailing behind, a prince riding along on a fox's tail, elves cavorting. The figures came from caricature. The raving, starveling Bonaparte he, Gillray and others had tormented on paper during the Napoleonic wars became an enraged Rumpelstiltskin stamping through the floor. Lord Castlereagh and other former government figures were lightly disguised as villains and fools. Ruskin, who enjoyed the book as a child, later described the illustrations as 'the finest things next to Rembrandt that have been done since etching was invented'. That may be arguable; nevertheless, Cruikshank had succeeded in giving form to a whole new range of fairy-tale characters with such decisive wit that all subsequent representations either reflected his images and his creatures or, at the very least, took them into account. The next stage in the development of the fairy tale cult came with the emergence of Hans Andersen in the 1840s. Until then, Cruikshank's interpretation remained unrivalled.

Meanwhile, book illustration began to flourish. Before Cruikshank's time a frontispiece was the most that was deemed necessary to adorn respectable fiction. But widening demand, as literacy spread, demonstrated that illustrations could popularize books out of all proportion to the costs involved. So Cruikshank illustrated the 'standard novels', including *Don Quixote* and *Robinson Crusoe* and the lighter side of Sir Walter Scott. His name began to supplant the author's on title pages: texts became little more than excuses for his illustrations. In 1828 he recorded every move in a complete Punch and Judy performance, a comic-strip scenario published in book form. Words dwindled into captions. He freed himself from any obligation to meet the authors' demands half-way by venturing into publishing on his own account with albums of etchings, *Phrenological Illustrations, Illustrations of Time* and *Scraps and Sketches*, and a *Comic Alphabet* (8) which unfolded into a long strip.

Cruikshank's etchings are nothing like as spontaneous as they appear. They were evolved from bundles of sketches and old caricature routines. Although they have no narrative structure, each image is equivalent to a page of dialogue, a paragraph of description or a single limerick. They were not intended for children but for family amusement; though Thackeray recalled 'forgoing tarts to buy his "Breaking Up"', clubbing together with his schoolfriends to get a copy of *Phrenological Illustrations* and then splitting the album up, reducing it to broadsheets.

Cruikshank's influence was already on the wane when in 1835, with Goethe's encouragement, Rudolphe Töpffer's *Histoire de Monsieur Jabot* was published in Paris. Töpffer's strips were the antitheses of Cruikshank's albums, not so much because they told stories but because Töpffer had no expertise to speak of, only enthusiasm (the 'all in all', as Blake said).

'He who uses drawings will have an advantage over those who talk in chapters,' Töpffer wrote in his *Essay on Physiognomy* in 1845. He drew his first 'histoire en estampes' in 1827 for his pupils at the school he ran in Geneva. Details would have blocked the flow of events, tonal refinements would have confused them. Töpffer employed direct means, a shorthand manner for speed and convenience, lithography because it was more straightforward than other methods of reproduction. But this was all to the good, for it meant that in his hands narrative shook off the usual ties of text and settings, 'finish' and 'finesse': Cruikshank's encumbrances.

Töpffer's stories were plagiarized (his *Monsieur Vieux-Bois*, for instance, was reborn as *Mr Obadiah Oldbuck*) and so his style, if not so much his name, became all the more widely propagated. Seen against the background of the more genteel children's publications of the 1830s – the *Tales of Peter Parley* (which, begun by Samuel Goodrich in Boston in 1827, was the first children's Annual) and the unrelievedly prissy *Juvenile Scrapbook* and its like, with steel engravings of winsome vistas and little ones bearing cherries – Töpffer's amateurism was more than refreshing; it was a way of escape.

Scrapbooks proper were another way of bypassing the conventional publications. Here illustrations were redeployed, reconstituted. They were put together on three levels, nursery, schoolroom and drawingroom, but were more or less interchangeable because they used the same materials: billheads, pinpackets (these were decorated with some of the earliest mass-produced colour prints), Bible scenes, plates from Cruikshank's *Comic Almanack*, Christmas cards (these began in the 1840s), jokes and engravings from the new illustrated papers. Scrapbooks were full of reminders, surprises, curious juxtapositions of style and image. They were source books, reference collections.

In December 1844 Dr Heinrich Hoffmann bought a blank exercise book for his son. 'I went to town with the intention to buy as a present for him a picture-book . . . but what did I find? Long tales, stupid collections of pictures, moralizing stories, beginning and ending with admonitions like: "the good child must be truthful", or "children must keep clean", etc.' Instead of handing the book over to be filled with scraps, Hoffmann wrote and drew *Struwwelpeter* in the beguiling bedside manner he had already evolved when trying to amuse his child patients.

The 'Pretty Stories and Funny Pictures' of *Struwwelpeter* were designed, not to horrify, but to entertain in grotesque exaggeration of the ordinary stricture books of the time. Hoffmann's ideas are spelt out, primarily, in the drawings: the hideous snip of the scissors (9), the red slippers that are all that remains of Harriet after she plays with the matches, and the title picture of Peter with his mane of hair and trailing fingernails, exhibited on a platform, a ridiculous Awful Warning (7).

Hoffmann insisted that his books should be loosely bound; for 'Children's books are here to be pulled to pieces'. *Struwwelpeter* evolved as it passed through a hundred editions in thirty years. Besides the parody versions of the book (in itself a spoof), the illustrations changed considerably from one edition to the next. The settings grew more elaborate. Hoffmann's original wispy figures were plumped out and solidified, but their spirit survived. Details were mere extras, easily pruned; the poses and gestures, the simple outlines of each character, were all that really counted.

Edward Lear's *Book of Nonsense* began as performances for the amusement of the Earl of Derby's children at Knowsley. In his role as the 'Old Derry down Derry, who loved to see little folks merry', he made drawings that evoked a child's-eye view of his professional work, a highly correct manner turned turtle. As he drew he made up the limericks – a quick verse form he remembered from John Marshall's *Anecdotes and Adventures of Fifteen Gentlemen*, which he had read when he was eight. Each one, with its formal introduction, event, consequence and verdict, is a peep at an extraordinary specimen; each one perches, nests, or struts about in courtship display, just like the toucans and parrots and other exotic birds Lear normally drew for a living. Occasionally glimpses of his usual clear-cut landscape style appear, in the temples of Philae behind the 'scroobious and wily Old Person' thereof, and Mount Etna, into which the Old Person of Gretna inevitably falls. In 1846 when the *Book of Nonsense* was published, Lear's rhymes underlined his drawings and emphasized their pace. Later on, in *Nonsense Songs* (1870) and *Laughable Lyrics* (1877), the images (the Owl and the Pussy Cat, the Jumblies) became essentially literary. Even the Dong with a Luminous Nose is somehow belittled when illustrated.

In 1848 *Il Pentamerone*, a collection of Neapolitan folk tales made by Giambattista Basile two hundred years before, was published in its first English edition, illustrated by Cruikshank in his intricate, slightly fussy, mature style (18). The edginess of *German Popular Stories* had given way to an ornate virtuosity.

By this time Cruikshank's invention was flagging, though his ingenuity never deserted him and his influence persisted, in the images of petit-bourgeois royalty in Thackeray's *Rose and the Ring* (19), in Doyle's elfin drollery (17), and in Leech's

Edward Lear
'The Dong with a Luminous Nose', from *Laughable Lyrics*, London 1877

illustrations to Gilbert à Beckett's parody-histories (15). These artists and writers were all connected with *Punch* which, founded in 1841, had taken over many of Cruikshank's targets and much of his public. Cruikshank refused to have anything to do with the paper, turned back to his private enterprises, and became teetotal, revising his imagery accordingly. He crammed his *Fairy Library* with teeming illustrations, many of them as charming as ever. But his moralizing asides and temperance happy endings brought protests from Dickens. In an article 'Frauds on Fairies' he complained 'half-playfully and half-seriously' that Cruikshank was despoiling childhood memories.

These were sacred to Dickens both in his autobiographical, *David Copperfield* moods and in his misty-eyed *Old Curiosity Shop* vein, in which he wrote of 'the laughing light and life of childhood, the gaiety that has known no check, the frankness that has felt no chill, the hope that has never withered, the joys that fade in blossoming'. Little Nell, to whom this refers, rose from her deathbed and, as the model for heroines of countless reward books and picture books, haunted childhood imagery for a generation. As Dickens described her, and George Cattermole represented her in the illustrations, she looked frail against the dark corruption of London, shone as she tended Mrs Jarley's grotesque waxworks, and lay angelic in death. *The Old Curiosity*

J. W. North
'Winter',
from *Touches of Nature*,
London and New York
c. 1860

SWAIN, Sc.

Noel Paton
Illustration to Charles Kingsley's
The Water Babies,
London 1863

Shop was written in 1840 and after that the cult of childhood, associated with nostalgic rural parts, became endemic. If babies are cherubs, the theory went, then little girls are angels and angels are fairies and fantasy a form of spiritual rebirth. There was a great demand for paintings of fairies, which smart painters, Noel Paton in particular, hastened to satisfy.

In Kingsley's *The Water Babies* of 1863, which Paton illustrated, all the childhood-cult themes were cunningly interwoven: Tom the chimney-sweep escaping from soot and smoke into picturesque countryside, drowning and passing through oblivion into a fairy aquarium. Paton's outline engravings evoke the book's muddled, chilly passion and its implication that there are only two ways to treat a child: to drool over it or to beat it.

Illustrations and all, *Alice's Adventures in Wonderland*, published two years later, was an immense improvement on Kingsley and Paton; although some of Lewis Carroll's introductory remarks surpassed even Dickens's Little Nellery: 'To be read? Nay, not so!... Say rather to be thumbed, to be cooed over, to be dog's-eared, to be rumpled, to be kissed by the illiterate, ungrammatical, dimpled Darlings.' Tenniel's stalwart illustrations irradiate the text. He treats Alice as a lifelike wax doll and the other characters as though they were ingenious clockwork models, probably German in origin. In *Alice Through the Looking Glass* Tenniel's contribution was even more vital.

The White Queen's whalebone crinoline, the White Knight's troublesome equipment, the identical Tweedledum and Tweedledee, are memorable because they are presented as though true to life. 'After that,' Tenniel later wrote to Carroll, 'the faculty of drawing for book illustration departed from me.' He spent the rest of his career doing political cartoons for *Punch* in the same literal-minded way.

Gustave Doré's exhaustive, often over-elaborate approach to fantasy is comparable to Tenniel's. His Rabelaisian illustrations to *Perrault's Fairy Tales* are less successful than the gimcrack Grand-Guignol of *Don Quixote* (1863, 22) and *The Adventures of Baron Munchhausen*. Doré should have illustrated Jules Verne's *Journey to the Centre of the Earth* and *From the Earth to the Moon*, both published at that time.

Doré started out as a caricaturist, but developed increasingly solemn tendencies as a book illustrator, and ended up painting vast Bible scenes. Wilhelm Busch was content to remain a designer of comic-cuts throughout his working life, contributing to the *Münchener Bilderbogen* (a broadsheet begun in 1849). 'Pictures', he said, 'come before words.' He made a speciality of cockroach brats, forever creeping into trouble and suffering appalling slapstick punishments. *Max und Moritz* (20) and *Naughty Jemima* were timely antidotes to the excesses of the childhood-wonderland cult. Busch's work has never been popular outside Germany, although his influence on the caricature tradition in children's illustration was as great as Töpffer's and comparable to Cruikshank's.

During the 1860s colour printing became dominant in the picture-book trade. Doré's black and white immensities began to look old-fashioned; Lear's Nonsense was reissued in coloured editions alongside an abundance of Birthday Books, Peeps at Nature and Historical Tableaux. In these the artists and authors generally sheltered behind names like Aunt Louisa, Aunt Judy or Tante Amiada (14), and the colouring was often plush and clotted, being intended to make each engraving look like an old master. James Doyle's *Chronicle of England*, in its neo-Domesday Book binding, is an extreme example of the 1860s gift volume, designed to be looked through with clean hands and adult supervision on Sunday afternoon. While the illustrations are rather stilted in outline (Doyle was a heraldic expert), the luminous colouring was an extraordinary achievement by the printer Edmund Evans. A few years later Evans's engravings for Richard Doyle's *In Fairyland* (17) showed, even more clearly, that it was possible to use colour with great subtlety. Instead of stifling the images with over-complicated printing, he used colour strategically, as the basis of composition.

Evans's most important collaborations, with Walter Crane, Randolph Caldecott and Kate Greenaway, directed children's illustration from narrative and caricature (the Cruikshank, Lear modes) into design.

Walter Crane admitted that his 'toy books' were 'the vehicle of my ideas in furniture and decoration'. He perfected a pure but eclectic manner; the dinner table scene in *The Frog Prince* (23), for example, contains hints of Botticelli and of Flaxman Neo-Classicism, and the sideboard is laden with blue and white japonaiserie. The relentless patterning in Crane's compositions, the firm outlines, the sense of occasions arranged into wallpaper friezes, made him a byword for stylish quality. For the first time children's books served as a design index, listing suitable looks (Crane's heroines tend to resemble Michelangelo's David) and modes. One could assume that every item he showed was available from Liberty's shop in Regent Street.

Working in black and white, Crane was little more than an outer ripple of the Pre-Raphaelite movement. In colour, however, he was an original, and sustained by Evans's printing skills he proved that he could sell enough books to make a profit, despite the fact that his sort of picture book was complicated and expensive to produce and yet sold at a low price.

From 1888 onwards Crane became a leading figure in the Arts and Crafts Movement. He also worked for a while with William Morris at the Kelmscott Press: for both, illustration was a means of spreading the ideal of an 'Earthly Paradise' attainable through the craftsman's skills and the artist's vision.

To Kate Greenaway and her admirers – George Eliot, for one, declared herself 'much charmed', and Ruskin was almost lost for words to express his delight – paradise was sometime securely in the past, the period perhaps of Blake's *Songs of Innocence*, or of Isaac Taylor's *Little Tarry-at-Home Travellers* (5), sweetened, however, and prettified in retrospect. Her Greenaway look first appeared in Christmas card designs and suddenly became famous when Edmund Evans took a batch of her poems and drawings, transformed the lines and washes into woodblocks and had them published by Routledge as *Under the Window* in 1878. The entire first edition of twenty thousand copies sold immediately and the look became a cult, a mode of dress imposed on a generation of children. Setting aside the obvious appeal of mob-capped infants playing adult in model villages, Kate Greenaway's success depended on her refreshed air, her apple-blossom and moss-green colour schemes.

Randolph Caldecott's *Shilling Picture Books* were also printed by Evans and published by Routledge from 1878 to 1885. He illustrated many of the same songs and nursery rhymes as Kate Greenaway but in a far more robust style. His russet-tinted Worcestershire (24) was the sort of countryside Rowlandson had enjoyed and that had persisted in rural idyll illustrations, tidied still further and made presentable for children.

The Crane, Greenaway and Caldecott picture books had an immediate effect. They lightened the prevailing tone in colour illustration and contributed to the spread of the international style which variously manifested itself as Arts and Crafts, Stile Liberty, Jugendstil and Art Nouveau. The labels overlap so much they hardly matter: the characteristics were more significant. These involved a general reaction against the florid chromo-lithography effects rampant, in Germany especially, towards the end of the century. In Munich Ernst Kreidolf made his own colour lithographs for *Blumenmärchen* (1898), comparable to Crane's *Flora's Feast* of 1889, and *Fitzebutze* (1900), demonstrating that the illustrator could do better without intermediary craftsmen. Ordinary school primers became elegant (43). Everyday scenes in Sweden (36) and the English home counties (31) and on Crusoe's desert island (40) were imbued with Arts and Crafts and Garden Suburb design principles. They were reproduced, however, by labour-saving methods, for by the 1880s photo-engraving had given the artist freedom to draw with hardly a thought for the printer. Hence there was a glut of folk-tale illustrations in the complex Burne-Jones idiom from J. D. Batten, H. J. Ford and others. Howard Pyle, acclaimed by fellow countrymen as the New World's answer to Walter Crane, illustrated his own quoth-and alack-ful stories with drawings that often appeared to be oaken-hearted versions of Kelmscott Press wood engravings (35).

Caldecott's cordial Old England had a counterpart in the misted France which Boutet de Monvel illustrated in several patriotic albums. De Monvel absorbed a swarm of influences, from French popular lithographs to Japanese prints. He presented *Jeanne d'Arc* (30) with much pageantry in a fin-de-siècle Uccello style. Like A. Hermant Job, whose *Le Bon Roy Henry* had a similarly spacious mood, he used lithography with great subtlety and restraint, alternating the heraldic glamour of daylight raids with empurpled stretches of night. In Russia, Ivan Bilibin exploited lithography to the utmost, with gilt highlights and superabundant textures, scenes half-buried in hieroglyphic borders (38). His illustrations to the Builini folk tales, retold by Pushkin, were equivalent in impact to the pre-war Russian ballet and came, perhaps, as final proof that from then on wood engraving was to be nothing more than a revivalist technique. But each new process demanded stylistic concessions. Even half-tone

Ernst Kreidolf
Illustration to Paula and Richard Dehmel's
Fitzebutze, Munich 1900

engraving, which in theory could reproduce any effect the black and white illustrator chose, imposed disciplines. Maxfield Parrish, notably, learnt to modify his designs. In his illustrations to Kenneth Grahame's *The Golden Age* (33) he viewed childhood through grey, characteristic half-tone mists, while keeping outlines and shadows distinct. He once described himself as 'a mechanic who paints'.

The four-colour process emerged at the turn of the century as the alternative to lithography, especially convenient for reproducing watercolours. As Beatrix Potter and Arthur Rackham demonstrated, this method bypassed most of the problems of nuance which had so beset the wood engravers. But as the process involved printing on shiny art paper, book design had to change to accommodate it. A special format evolved with tipped-in plates, and everything possible was done to make a virtue of the clumsy interleaving of art paper and thicker letterpress pages. Arthur Rackham, Edmund Dulac, W. Heath Robinson and his brother Charles, N. C. Wyeth, Kay Nielsen and Howard Pyle, in his later years, provided a wealth of sturdy detail, jewelled fancies, startling perspectives and, when the occasion arose, piquant (but generally mermaid) nudity. Rackham, in particular, developed a near-patent technique suited to the process which involved swamping his drawings with dim tones, then accentuating the contrasts between gnarled trees, weathered buildings and ethereal, ivory-complexioned girls. He was at his best in *Peter Pan in Kensington Gardens* (1906), Edward VII taking the air, with magic afoot (48). Dulac minimized the risk of distortion in reproduction with a quasi-Persian miniature style. He was most successful when illustrating the cruel slights and vainglories of *Stories from Hans Andersen* (57). Many of these gift volumes were handsome – but compared with the de Monvel and Bilibin albums they were mere production numbers, more show than substance, and the lesser examples were full of sub-Bakst mannerisms and Isadora Duncan fairies.

While these luxury books passed way beyond most children's grasp, other more available forms of illustration emerged. Heath Robinson and Rackham did much of their early work for cheap magazines and annuals. Free advertising stickers and cigarette cards, cadged from adults, could be collected and stuck in albums: heroes, landmarks, badges, first-aid tips, curiosities and inventions in batches of fifty or more (53, 54, 55). Picture postcards supplied a new form of topography for 'Little Tarry-at-Home Travellers'. Busch and Hoffmann pranksters re-emerged in the comic strips and ran amok among the wonders of modern times (41); most dramatically Winsor McCay's *Little Nemo* (45), who wandered nightly inside his fully-furnished imagination, confusing men and animals and live and inanimate objects. Sometimes his bed stretched its legs and walked. Comedy policemen, prototype Keystone Cops, hustled him off. Blackamoors grimaced. Beardsley underworlds, Sant' Elia skyscrapers, Méliès backdrops bewildered him, the world shrank. But in the last frame he always woke up to find he had fallen out of bed and his mother was calling him for breakfast.

By the time *Little Nemo* started to appear in the *New York Herald* in 1905, dolls and toys, Noah's arks, railway sets, dolls' houses, lead soldiers, had become prominent in children's imagery (42). Children, unable to envisage themselves as adults in stories or illustrations (except in the most stereotyped roles of pirate, nurse, giant-killer), could identify with toys, bring them to life and treat them as humans. Animated playing cards and chess pieces had supplied half the characters in *Alice in Wonderland* and *Through the Looking Glass*. *Pinocchio*, first published around 1881, but best illustrated by Attilio Mussino (70) in 1924, changed from puppet into boy, grew donkey's ears and survived the whale's belly. Florence Upton invented the name Golliwog in 1898 and showed nursery figures dancing and fighting (37) in much the same style and spirit as de Monvel's historical figures. Similarly the characters who befriended Dorothy in the *Oz* stories were playthings turned into larger-than-life playmates (51).

Animals too had well-known characters: the sly fox and spry rabbit of the *Aesop* and *Uncle Remus* menageries (32), and the political cartoon figures – British lion, Russian bear, German eagle – always reacted as expected. Similarly, Benjamin Rabier's animals (starting in the 1880s) were put through behaviourist music hall routines (60). Leslie Brooke established an animal kingdom in stately garden settings (46), each creature acting more or less traditionally. Children could half-anticipate their antics, thus saving authors and illustrators a great deal of trouble conveying character. Animals masked humans (92). Ernest Shepard, for instance, envisaged Mole, Rat and Toad as thoroughly Edwardian Thames Valley types (82) and Krazy Kat, whose frustrated escapades began in 1910, was nothing more than a roaming ego.

Beatrix Potter's animals, drawn with something of Ruskin's devotion to detail, Caldecott's charm, Hosemann's fantasy (14) and Bewick's intensity, originated in the study of her pets and stuffed specimens at the Natural History Museum in South Kensington. Though she dramatized them and dressed them up, she never distorted her creatures. Occasionally, when she introduced humans – such as herself going to post a letter at the end of *Samuel Whiskers* – she struck a false note. But most of the time she focused on the animals, each illustration a nature vignette (50). Her storyteller's trimmings were always mildly cautionary, sometimes, as in *The Tailor of Gloucester* and *The Tale of Mr Tod*, almost Dickensian. The pictures mirrored the words but always seized the attention first so that the text had to catch up, explaining and commenting.

In the original editions the format of the books varied considerably. Some were chapbooks in scale, others almost novelettes, and she intended *The Sly Old Cat, The Fierce Bad Rabbit* and *The Tale of Miss Moppet* to be panoramas, unfolding like Cruikshank's *Comic Alphabet*, with few words needed.

By the end of the First World War the Potter era was virtually over, for after her marriage in 1913 she devoted herself to hill-farming and the stories virtually ceased, though her influence persisted. Heath Robinson, who did a series of gimcrack weaponry cartoons during the war, subsequently concentrated on being a comic artist. Rackham and Dulac contributed gift book illustrations to the war effort and, while no longer innovators, remained active and prestigious. Rackham was asked to help with his special wild wood and old witch effects on Disney's *Snow White and the Seven Dwarfs* in 1937, and Dulac produced a delicate and unexpectedly appropriate set of illustrations to *Treasure Island* in 1927.

But in the post-war publishing revival the most lively books appeared to be reactions against Dulac values. Edy Legrand's *Macao et Cosmage* (67) of 1919, brilliantly coloured by the hand-stencil, 'pochoir' process in a Jazz-Fauve manner, was a demonstration piece, illustrating the degradation of a paradise isle with the coming of civilization. In both this and *Voyages et glorieuses découvertes des grands navigateurs et explorateurs français* (1921), Legrand shook up the conventions of children's illustration. So did André Hellé in woodcut-style drawings for a modernized version of La Fontaine's *Fables* (62), while Jodel's *Napoléon* went still further back to the most basic popular tradition (72). The equivalent in Germany was K. F. von Freyhold's *Hasenbuch* (61), with its hints of Matisse. Modernism now meant avoiding the four-colour process.

With the invention of educational psychology, the registration of reading ages and intelligence quotients and the growth of public libraries, especially in the United States where the *Horn Book Magazine* was begun in 1924, children's books were more in demand and, probably, more severely scrutinized than ever. *Struwwelpeter* fell into disrepute, *Alice in Wonderland* was analysed. Comics were deplored. Worthiness won awards.

Some of the best illustrations of the 1920s, and the least assuming, were Hugh Lofting's drawings of Doctor Dolittle (64), a portly Crusoe anticipating Thurber's Mitty menfolk, and the lightning character studies done by the cartoonist Walter Trier for Erich Kästner's *Emil and the Detectives* in 1929. Occasionally experiment became radical – as in the knockabout New Typography of the two little books Kurt Schwitters produced with Theo van Doesburg and Kate Steinitz in Hanover (76). But they were not commercially published and so went virtually unnoticed.

Yet styles and ideas spread more quickly and more widely than before. The oblong format and lithography of William Nicholson's *Clever Bill* of 1926 (followed by *The Pirate Twins*, 75) was admired and taken up by Wanda Gåg (85) in America. Roger Duvoisin, whose *A Little Boy was Drawing* was published in New York in 1932, Artzybasheff, Rojankovsky and Edgar Parain d'Aulaire moved from Europe to the United States. Like Maurice Sendak, more recently, they were link-figures. Feodor Rojankovsky, a Russian who worked in Paris during the early 1930s before settling in New York, was the most important. The large pages, strong colours and clever stylizations of his *Daniel Boone* (73), published simultaneously in Paris, London and New York in 1931, made a considerable impression, though at the *beau livre* end of the market. But he also did a number of splendid illustrations for Père Castor books, a series produced by a Parisian bookseller which eventually amounted to over two hundred and fifty titles and sold millions of copies. They were cheap, bright, calculatedly educational, and ranged from calendars and wild animal stories illustrated by Rojankovsky (84) to board-games and cut-out albums by Nathalie Parain (81), the other outstanding Père Castor artist. Some of her designs anticipated Matisse's *papiers-découpés*.

The equivalent to the Père Castor albums in Russia, and probably their inspiration, were paperbacks produced, as Maxim Gorky explained, on the principle that children's books should 'say what they have to say in an enjoyable manner so that children develop a sense of humour'. Folk tales and animal stories with witty, free-for-all illustrations were published in huge editions (probably a minimum of sixty thousand copies) to offset accounts of heroic industrial progress (83, 86).

In Germany the same movement towards cheaper, attractive, semi-educational books can be seen in the publications of the Herbert Stuffer Verlag: Marianne Scheel's illustrations of the farmer's year (79) and Friedrich Boer's largely photo-montage books about the workings of a town and a railway (78). With a few exceptions, like Sougez's dapper *Alphabet* of 1932 (77), photographs were little used in respectable children's books at this time partly, at least, because of the problems in colour reproduction and the idea that black and white photographs were somehow mundane, vulgar and too similar to rival cinematic attractions. But the books that generally failed to be mentioned on reading lists or bought by the public libraries abounded in photographs and often contained outstanding line drawings and colour plates. Bumper annuals and books about the marvels of electricity, the wonders of railways, aeroplanes and cars (74) all flaunted images of glamorous streamlining, speed, power, dauntless courage.

There were also new popular heroes who had little in common with Kay Nielsen's matinée idol princelings, Nicholson's *Velveteen Rabbit*, or E. H. Shepard's benign studies of *Winnie-the-Pooh*. Charlie Chaplin was taken down from the screen and put into comic strips. Laurel and Hardy followed, a child-generation later. And in the short time it took for Mickey Mouse to be invented and shaped into formula – a cross between the comic-strip Chaplin and Krazy Kat's constant assailant Ignatz Mouse – the limits of illustration were extended. Mickey Mouse first appeared in 1929 in *Plane Crazy*, soon rose to full colour, all-squeaking roles and, like Chaplin before him, began to feature in annuals and comics, the key figure in an ever-increasing cast of animal types.

When Walt Disney's ambition outgrew his *Silly Symphony* cartoon shorts, he took to the classics and reconstituted *Snow White* and *Pinocchio* in film form. These in turn led to books-of-the-films, strip cartoons and spin-off records with pop-up sleeves showing scenes from each production. Whatever debt Disney owed to the story of 'Snow-Drop' in *German Popular Stories*, to Rackham, Mussino and Benjamin Rabier, his became the most persistent, the most widely-appreciated version of the stories. The Disney copyright took over. The M.G.M. version of *The Wizard of Oz* also transcended L. Frank Baum's book and bypassed the original illustrations.

Ordinary, static comic strips could hardly compete with the films though Harold Foster's blend of Pyle and McCay in *Prince Valiant* was a formidable attempt to keep pace with Douglas Fairbanks. After a fumbling start in 1938, Superman too rose to become enduring but adaptable and, for this reason, seems likely to outlive the Disney creations who, while still going strong, are trapped by their trademarks in the pre-war era.

The most meticulous comic strip, Hergé's *Tintin* (89), which began in 1929, has survived because each story, crammed with local colour and passing jokes, is a rattling good pictorial yarn. Rupert the Bear, founded by Mary Tourtel in 1920, has slipped into a timeless childhood state, a Garden Suburban surrealism (92). The smash-and-grab characters of the *Dandy* and *Beano* comics have come to haunt the back streets. These strips are a form of journalism, evolving daily, imperishable only so long as the pace is sustained and the idea appeals. This is the basic difference

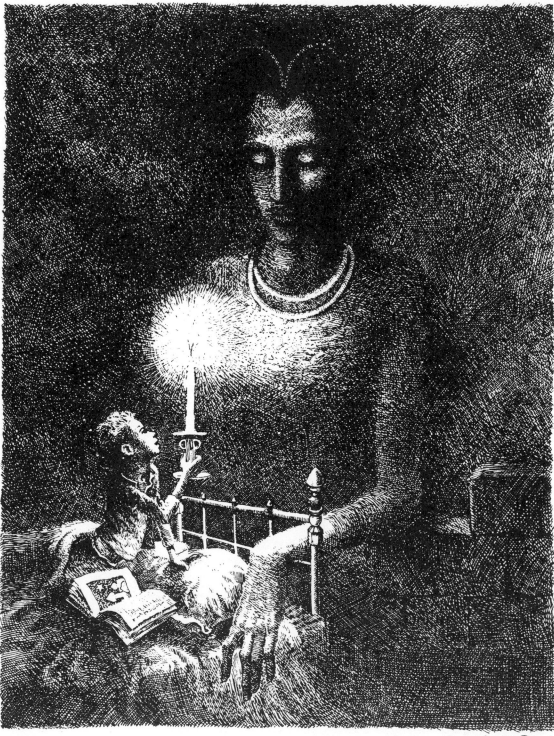

Mervyn Peake
'How many miles to Babylon?',
from *Ride a Cock Horse*,
London 1941

22

Maurice Sendak 'The juniper tree', from *The Juniper Tree and Other Tales from Grimm*, London 1973

between a cartoon figure like Mickey Mouse, who is essentially an arrangement of pouncing gestures, and the true picture book characters like Babar, Orlando or Little Tim.

Jean de Brunhoff wrote only six Babar stories. The continuations by his son Laurent have not so much added to the œuvre as distracted; so have the subsequent reprocessed, scaled-down and fragmented editions of the books. In the original, folio-size versions, the graphic coups were frequent: the first appearance of the Old Lady, busy holiday brochure landscapes seen from ship, skis or balloon, the rout of the rhinos, Babar's gradual assumption of authority over his Peaceable Kingdom and regal trappings (94). Comparable books, notably Pierre Noury's *Le Prince Toto Che* (90), were around at the time the first Babar books appeared, but none were illustrated with such imperturbable grace.

Edward Ardizzone's *Little Tim* (96) went through a series of adventures at sea from 1936 into the 1960s. His staying power rested on his uncannily resourceful character and on Ardizzone's way with storms, snug cabins, spells of golden sunset calm, sketched in a spontaneous and unfussed style. Kathleen Hale, by contrast, delights in ornate, often punning detail. She designed her first Orlando book as an English equivalent to Babar, the same format and comparable story.

Several mechanical heroes emerged during the late 1930s. Jan Lewitt and George Him's *Locomotywa* (93), in impeccable streamlined style, was first published in Poland. After settling in London they began a series of stories about *The Little Red Engine*, later illustrated, in similar panoramic manner, by Leslie Wood (100). Virginia Lee Burton's *Mike Mulligan and his Steam Shovel* and *The Little House* (99) were arranged page by page, time and distances folding past, like dissolving views.

Puffin Picture Books, founded by Noel Carrington during the war, were an extension of the paperback tradition established in Russia and France and, to begin with, included stories, among them *Orlando's Evening Out* (102). Later the series became wholly instructive, covering topics from *Trees* and the *Battle of Britain* to *Printing* and *Living Pictures*. Margaret and Alexander Potter made the lithographs for their brisk *History of the Countryside* (101) on the kitchen table in a wartime agricultural hostel. The rather improvised, emergency appearance of several of these Puffins added to their charms.

But illustration is more than a means of conveying instruction. 'There must be above all things the power to slide into another man's soul,' Mervyn Peake said. The illustrator has to arouse curiosity, set scenes, spark off reactions. In *Ride a Cock Horse* Peake looked down on childhood but somehow failed to make contact. Yet in his illustrations to *Treasure Island* he reacted as a child might to the storming of the stockade (107), turning Stevenson's paragraph into a recurrent-nightmare image. Edward Burra's illustrations to *Huckleberry Finn* (103) have the same fixated quality; so, in a milder, more insidious way, have Harold Jones's lithographs in *This Year: Next Year* (95).

Children's illustrations serve many ends. They furnish memories, convey fantasies, help the eye skip through Blyton adventures. As the traditions lengthen, the stockpile of imagery accumulates and mannerisms come and go in cycles. But the demands hardly change: Hoffmann, Lear, Busch, Crane, Rackham and Potter remain in print. 'I want! I want!' children have gone on shouting. In 1950, where, for perspective's sake, this survey ends, Dan Dare was on the cover of a pop-up book, floating in space, somewhere beyond the moon.

Frank Hampson
Cover of *Dan Dare: Pilot of the Future*, London *c.* 1950

LONDON

I wander thro' each charter'd street,
Near where the charter'd Thames does flow
And mark in every face I meet
Marks of weakness, marks of woe.

In every cry of every Man,
In every Infants cry of fear,
In every voice: in every ban,
The mind-forg'd manacles I hear

How the Chimney-sweepers cry
Every blackning Church appalls,
And the hapless Soldiers sigh
Runs in blood down Palace walls

But most thro' midnight streets I hear
How the youthful Harlots curse
Blasts the new-born Infants tear
And blights with plagues the Marriage hearse

2 **Anonymous** *'The stubborn child'* 1800

3 **Thomas Bewick** *Children playing on tombstones* 1797

5 **Anonymous** *'Cheviot Shepherds;*
Bamburgh Castle; Berwick upon Tweed' 1821

4 After **William Mulready**
'Who with him the Wasp, his companion, did bring,
But they promis'd that ev'ning to lay by their sting' 1807

6 **Thomas Bewick** *'The crow and the pitcher'* 1818

7 **Heinrich Hoffmann**
'Shock-headed Peter' c. 1900 ▷

1. Shock=Headed Peter.

Just look at him! There he stands,
With his nasty hair and hands.
See! his nails are never cut;
They are grim'd as black as soot;
And the sloven, I declare,
Never once has comb'd his hair;
Any thing to me is sweeter
Than to see Shock-headed Peter.

8 **George Cruikshank** Letters from the *Comic Alphabet* 1836

9 **Heinrich Hoffmann**
' "*Ah!*" *said Mamma,* "*I knew he'd come
To naughty little Suck-a-Thumb*" ' *c.* 1876

There was an Old Man of the Hague, whose ideas were excessively vague;
He built a balloon to examine the moon,
That deluded Old Man of the Hague.

There was an Old Man who said, "Hush! I perceive a young bird in this bush!"
When they said, "Is it small?" he replied, "Not at all!
It is four times as big as the bush!"

Edward Lear 'There was an Old Man of the Hague' and
'There was an Old Man who said "Hush!"' 1870

11　**John Martin** *'The Third Temptation'* 1835

12　**Rudolphe Töpffer** *Doctor Festus appoints vigilantes to keep watch on a flying telescope* 1840

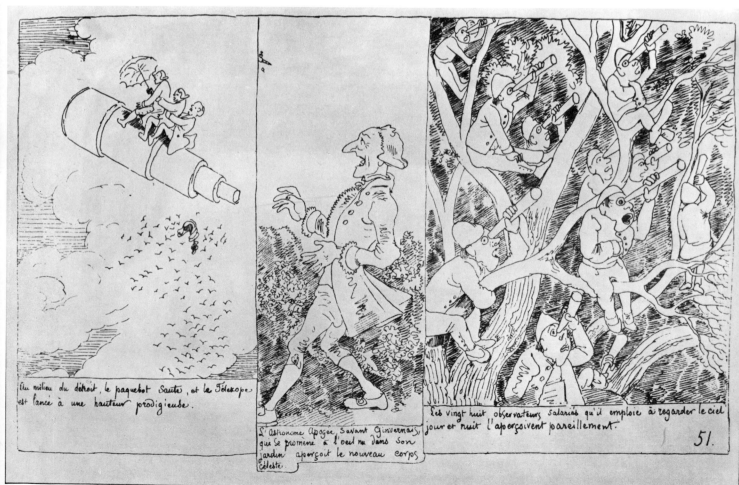

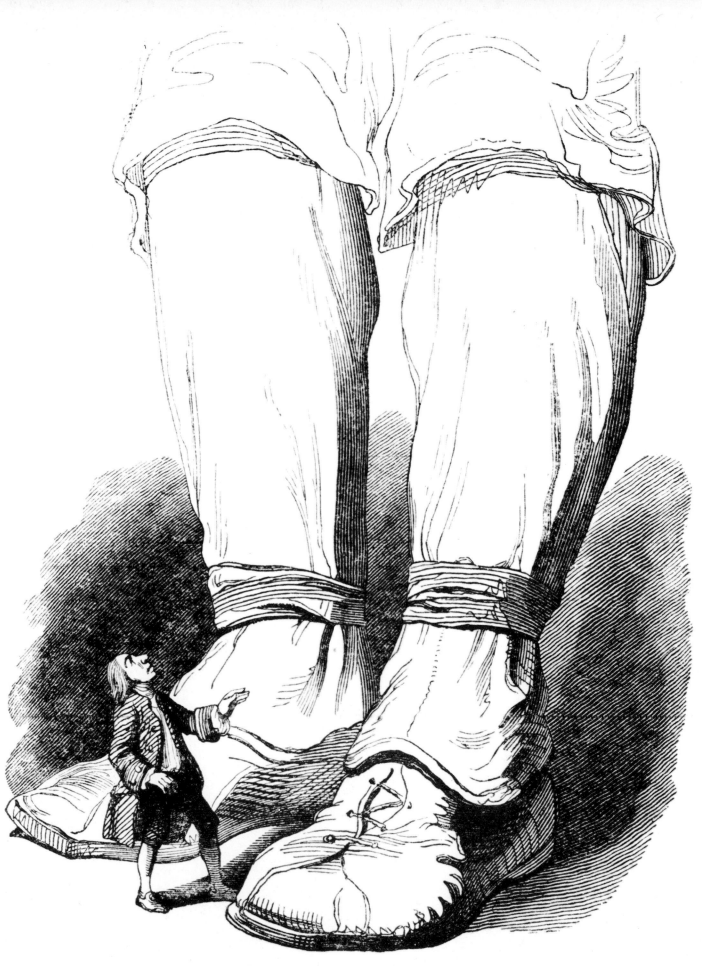

13 **Grandville (Jean-Ignace Gérard)**
Gulliver in Brobdingnag 1840

14 **Theodore Hosemann** *Hare towed away by ducks* 1872

15 **John Leech** *'The landing of Julius Caesar'* 1847

16 **James E. Doyle**
'The murder of the Duke of Suffolk, 1450' 1864

17 **Richard Doyle** *'The Elf-King asleep'* 1870

20 Wilhelm Busch
'Up goes a chicken!'
1865

18 George Cruikshank
'Peruonto riding on the faggot past the palace'
and *'Vardiello chasing the cat'* 1848

19 William Makepeace Thackeray
'Bulbo led away (weeping) to execution' 1855

21 Richard Doyle
'South-West Wind, Esq., knocking at the
Black Brothers' door' 1851

22   **Gustave Doré** '*The sail hurled away both knight and horse along with it*' 1863

23 **Walter Crane**
'The Princess shares her dinner with the frog'
1874

24   Randolph Caldecott
'Sing a song for sixpence,
A pocketful of rye,
Four-and-twenty blackbirds
Baked in a pie'
1880

25   Kate Greenaway
'Hark! hark! the dogs bark'
1881

Hark! hark! the dogs bark,
The beggars are coming to town;
Some in rags and some in tags,
And some in silken gowns.
Some gave them white bread,
And some gave them brown,
And some gave them a good horse-whip,
And sent them out of the town.

26 **Moritz von Schwind** *Puss in Boots makes his master's fortune* 1850

27 John Tenniel
'The Mad Hatter's Tea Party'
1865

28 John Tenniel
'Alice and the White Queen'
1871

29 Walter Crane
*'There she found poor Beast
stretched out, quite senseless'*
1875

30 **M. Boutet de Monvel**
Joan of Arc : the Battle of Patay
1896

31 **Francis Bedford**
'*The village store*'
1899

Le 18 juin, Jeanne atteignit, près de Patay, l'armée anglaise con-
duite par Talbot et Falstaff.

« En nom Dieu il faut les combattre, dit-elle ; quand ils seraient
pendus aux nues, nous les aurons, parce que Dieu nous les envoie
pour que nous les châtiions. Notre gentil Roi aura aujourd'hui la
plus grande victoire qu'il eut. » Elle voulait se porter à l'avant-garde,
on la retint, et La Hire fut chargé d'attaquer les Anglais pour les
obliger à faire volte-face, afin de donner aux troupes françaises le
temps d'arriver. Mais l'attaque de La Hire fut si impétueuse que
tout céda devant lui. Lorsque Jeanne accourut avec ses hommes
d'armes, les Anglais se retiraient en désordre. Leur retraite devint
une fuite. Talbot fut pris.

« Vous ne pensiez pas ce matin que cela vous arriverait », lui dit
le duc d'Alençon. « C'est la fortune de la guerre », répondit Talbot.

32 A. B. Frost
Brer Bear acts frightening
1895

33 Maxfield Parrish *'It was easy . . . to transport yourself in a trice to the heart of a tropical forest'* 1899

34 Ernest Griset *'The return home'* c. 1880

35 **Howard Pyle** *'Little John in ye guise of a friar stops three lasses'* 1883

36 **Carl Larsson** *A bedtime scene* 1904

37 **Florence K. Upton**
'And now the Ball is at its height,
A madly whirling throng'
1898

Ivan A. Bilibin *Ivan the Crown Prince* 1899

39 **W. Heath Robinson**
'Uncle Lubin was able to start on his voyage' 1902

40 **John Hassall**
'Crusoe and his pets at meal times' c. 1900

41 **Lyonel Feininger** 'The Kin-der-Kids Relief-Expedition' 1906

42 **W. Heath Robinson** '*The Battle*' 1904   43 **Max Dasio** Page from a school primer *c.* 1900

44 **Willy Pogany** '*They came at length to Mount Fuji*' 1915

Winsor McCay 'Little Nemo in Slumberland' 1908

But the Giraffe
Was inclined to laugh;

Leslie Brooke
'*But the Giraffe*
Was inclined to laugh' 1907

48 **Arthur Rackham**
'*The Kensington Gardens are in London,*
where the King lives'
1906

47 **N. C. Wyeth** '*Sir Mador's spear brake*
all to pieces, but the other's spear held'
1920

49 **N. C. Wyeth**
'*The Battle at Glens Falls*'
1920

50 Beatrix Potter
'Benjamin, on the contrary, was perfectly at home, and ate a lettuce leaf'
1904

51 John R. Neill
'The stranger removed his hat with a flourish'
1904

THE STRANGER REMOVED HIS HAT WITH A FLOURISH.

52 **Arthur Rackham** *'At the dead time of the night in came the Welsh giant'* 1916

53 Ogden's 'Guinea Gold' cigarette cards: *Mabel Roma* c. 1894,
'Lieut.-Gen. Baden-Powell' 1911, *'Statue to Mr Kruger in Pretoria'* 1900

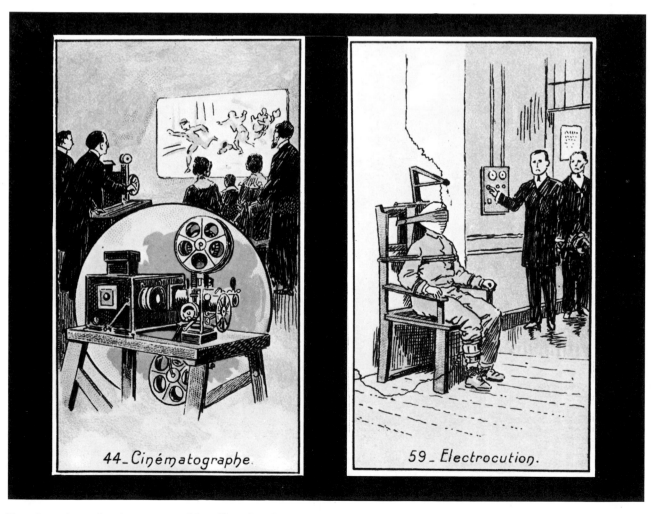

54 French trade cards, given away with coffee, showing
the wonders of electricity

Tennis

Iª WEINESSIG
MARKE: WEIBERTREU
GEORG FRIEDRICH RUND
HEILBRONN A/N.

Athletik
Wrestling
Lutte

Musik
Music — Musique

Widmer's -Selbstroller
für
Landkarten u. Rouleaux

Turnen
Drill — Gymnastique

Steinstossen
Throwing
the hammer

Lancement du poids

Die praktischsten Rouleaux
Widmer's Selbstroller
mit
Widmer's Rouleaux-Stoffen

Feuerwehr
Firemen
Sapeurs-
pompiers

56 **Kay Nielsen**
'The Lad in Battle' 1914

57 **Edmund Dulac**
'I have hardly closed my eyes all night' 1912

58 **Edmund Dulac** *'The Palace of the Dragon King'* 1915

59 **Kay Nielsen** *Hansel and Gretel approaching the witch's gingerbread house in the forest* 1925

60 **Benjamin Rabier**
*'An odd character, or the
gander in his Sunday best'*
c. 1910

61 **K. F. von Freyhold**
*'The Easterhouse is
nearly ready'*
1920

LE LION ABATTU PAR L'HOMME

On exposait une peinture
où l'artisan avait tracé
un lion d'immense stature
par un seul homme terrassé.

André Hellé '*The lion knocked down by the man*' 1922

65 **Marcel de Vinck**
'*A great feast in which the whole tribe took part*' c. 1925

63 **O. Štáfl**
'*Little Tom found himself in a clock with a cuckoo and thought he was in an enchanted castle*' 1922

64 **Hugh Lofting**
'*An enormous footprint*'
1920

é à laquelle   assiste toute la tribu.

XXX

Patty-cake, patty-cake,
  Baker's man,
Bake me a cake
  As fast as you can.
Prick it and prick it,
  And mark it with a T,
And put it in the oven

66 **Claud Lovat Fraser**
'Patty-cake, patty-cake'
1922

67　**Edy Legrand** *Macao and Cosmage settle on their paradise island* 1919

LES ENFANTS IMPRUDENTS !....
NE JOUEZ PAS SUR LA CHAUSSÉE..

71 **Walter Trier**
'*Trude crowed like a singer,*
Arthur's arm got longer and longer' 1931

72 **Jodel**
(J. de Lalande)
'The coronation' c. 1925

73 **Feodor Rojankovsky**
*'In 1774 War was declared
on the Indian tribes'*
1931

74 **Leslie Carr**
'At the petrol station' c. 1930 ▷

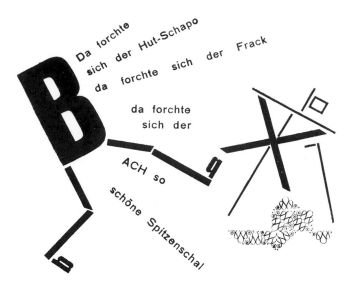

75 William Nicholson
'What "S" stands for'
1929

**76 Kurt Schwitters, Kate Steinitz,
Theo van Doesburg**
Letterplay with the New Typography 1925

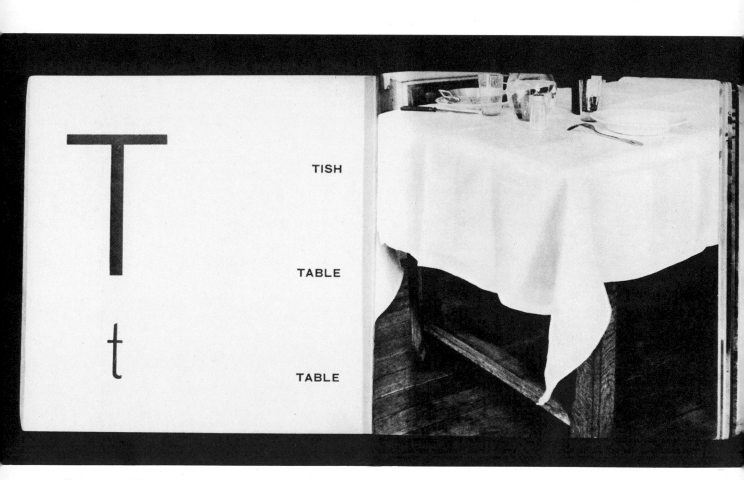

77 Emmanuel Sougez *'T Table'* 1932

Auf dem Bahnsteig ist viel los. Die Reisenden sehen aus dem Fenster oder stehen noch vor dem Zuge.
Und alle sind ein wenig aufgeregt.

Ein Professor blättert hastig in einem Kursbuch.

Ein junges Mädchen mit Rucksack und Stock sieht sich ruhig nach einem schönen Platz um. Bald ist sie weit weg in den Bergen.

Eine dicke Dame mit Hund und Vogelbauer, mit vielen Koffern und einem kleinen Jungen hat noch immer nicht alles Gepäck beisammen. — Ein anderer Junge erkundigt sich bei dem Aufsichtsbeamten.

12

78 **Friedrich Boer** *'On the platform'* 1933

79 **Marianne Scheel**
'October' 1934

80 **Anonymous**
The cat's house on fire
1937

IX. — L'ORAGE.

1. — (L'histoire commence ici). Le ciel est noir, un éclair brille.
Un tourbillon emporte le béret d'un écolier. Une petite fille s'accroche
craintivement à la robe de sa grand'mère. La pluie tombe. Quel orage !
Tout le monde court s'abriter.

82 **Ernest Shepard**
'*Mole and Rat load the picnic*'
1931

83 **Vladimir Lebedev**
*The poodle has wound wool round the old lady
and the cat* 1934

84   Feodor Rojankovsky
'February' : the jumping pancake
1936

85   Wanda Găg
'And they began to quarrel'
1928

86 **Vladimir Konashevich**
'*The cockroach*' 1935

87 **Garcin Jo**
'*The motorcar*'
1930

JE ME RAPPELLE BIEN ; J'APPUIE SUR LA
PÉDALE DE GAUCHE POUR DÉBRAYER, PUIS
JE PLACE LE LEVIER EN ARRIÈRE A GAUCHE.
— C'EST TRÈS BIEN, DIT LE PETIT MÉCANO,
JUSQU'ICI TU AS COMPRIS.
CRAC ROUGIT D'ORGUEIL ET TIMIDEMENT
IL APPUIE SUR LA PÉDALE DE L'ACCÉLÉRATEUR.
L'AUTO EST EN MARCHE.

— ALLONS, DIT LE PETIT MÉCANO, TU AS
LACHÉ TROP VITE LE DÉBRAYAGE ; IL FALLAIT LE
MAINTENIR UN PEU ET NE PAS L'ABANDONNER
COMME ÇA TOUT D'UN COUP.
L'AUTO AVANCE DOUCEMENT, MAIS CRAC
DÉCRIT DES ZIGZAGS SANS POUVOIR RESTER
DANS LA LIGNE DROITE.
LE PETIT MÉCANO N'EST PLUS TRÈS RAS-
SURÉ ; IL ESSAYE DE POSER UNE MAIN
PRUDENTE SUR LE VOLANT ET DÉJA IL
ORDONNE :
— ARRÊTE-TOI, TU NE SAIS PAS CON-
DUIRE.

Sonntagsausflug

88 **Elsa Moeschlin**
'*The Sunday outing*'
1933

89 **Hergé**
(Georges Rémi)
*Tintin: The Seven Crystal
Balls c.* 1938

90   Pierre Noury
Prince Toto : the final rout
1933

91   Boris Artzybasheff
'*King Douda welcomes Helena
to his kingdom*' 1937

92   Mary Tourtel
'*Rupert and the magician's
umbrella*' c. 1930

93   Jan Lewitt, George Him
The locomotive 1938

très content
de ses achats
et satisfait
de son élégance,
Babar va
chez le photographe.

_16_

94   **Jean de Brunhoff** *'Very happy with his shopping and pleased with his elegance, Babar*
goes to the photographer's' 1931

95 **Harold Jones**
'*Esmeralda*' 1937

would tell him about his voyages
and sometimes give him a sip of
his grog, which made Tim want to
be a sailor more than ever.

Edward Ardizzone '*When it was wet Tim would visit Captain McFee, who would tell him about his voyages and sometimes give him a sip of his grog, which made Tim want to be a sailor more than ever*' 1936

97 **Ernst Rüegg**
'*Then the first rainbow appears,*
and the sun shines again on
the rain-drenched fields' 1941

98 **Clarke Hutton**
'*Serge was upside down.*
His head looked through his hands
at the old man' 1943

99 **Virginia Lee Burton** *'One day the Little House was surprised to see a horseless carriage coming down the winding country road'* 1942

100 **Leslie Wood** *The little red engine* 1945

RIBBON DEVELOPMENT

With the twentieth century came the motor car and the motor bus. It made transport in and out of towns very easy and cheap. Everyone thought how much nicer it would be to live outside the town with a garden of your own and the countryside at your door. But the countryside was soon far away, because others went beyond you all the time. The builders put their houses along the roads because it saved making a new road and a bus ran past the door. This is called Ribbon Development. It has cut across the English landscape for miles outside every town and often joined several towns together. Eventually it proves to be a wasteful kind of development. The agricultural land is spoilt. The owners are far from shops, schools or cinemas. The road is dangerous for traffic and for children. It is neither town nor country. Ribbon building is now being stopped.

Margaret and Alexander Potter
'Ribbon development' 1943

"This Clever and Intrepid Cat, a stranger to us, has not only entertained us all with his marvellous performance, but has also saved the life of our dear Mr. Meek, the Lion-Tamer!"

"Bravo! Bravo!" bellowed the Audience.

"Therefore," he continued, "I have the honour of presenting him with a gold medal!"

The Orchestra played "For He's a Jolly Good Feline, and so say all of us!"

A spot light was turned on Orlando, who I'm afraid, wasn't listening. He was dealing with an over-excited flea which, tired of circus life on a tiger, wished for domestic peace on Orlando.

The Audience cheered and stamped, shouting "Speech! Speech!"

The kittens purred so loudly and so proudly that an attendant had to ask them to be quiet.

103 Edward Burra
*'The segars was prime. We laid off all the afternoon
in the woods talking, and me reading the books,
and having a general good time'*
1947

104 C. Walter Hodges *Columbus's transatlantic voyage* 1939

105 **Brian Robb** '*The ship struck with amazing force against (as we supposed) a rock*' 1947

106 **John Minton** '*Long John Silver*' 1947

107 **Mervyn Peake** *The storming of the stockade* 1949

108 **Maurice Sendak**
'*Mickey in Dough*'

Annotated List of Illustrations

1 **William Blake** (1757–1827)
Songs of Experience, London 1794
'London'. Hand-coloured relief etching.

Blake produced few copies of the book – perhaps two dozen. As a more commercial artist he adapted Daniel Chodowiecki's *Das Elementarwerk* (1774) for English publication in 1790, did engravings for Mary Wollstonecraft's *Original Stories from Real Life* (1791) and, most notably, made woodcuts for a school text, *Thornton's Virgil* (1820).

2 **Anonymous**
LADY FENN, *Cobwebs to Catch Flies* Vol. 2, printed by T. C. Hansard, London *c.* 1800 (n.d.)
'The stubborn child'
'Mr Steady was walking out with his little son, when he met a boy . . . sobbing dismally.
          MR STEADY
      Why do you cry?
          BOY
They send me to school, and I do not like it.'

The staid, catechismic method of writing and illustrating for children. The first version of the book, written by Lady Fenn, was published in 1783 under the full title: *Cobwebs to Catch Flies; or Dialogues in short sentences, adapted to children from the age of three to eight years.*

3 **Thomas Bewick** (1753–1828)
The History of British Birds Vol. 1, Newcastle upon Tyne 1797
Children playing on tombstones. Woodcut.

Bewick's vignettes, his 'tale pieces' as he called them, often contain *memento mori*: children playing beside gibbets, skulls, gravestones.

4 after **William Mulready** (1786–1863)
W. ROSCOE, *The Butterfly's Ball, and the Grasshopper's Feast*, London 1807
   'Who with him the Wasp, his companion, did bring,
   But they promis'd that ev'ning to lay by their sting'

Mulready later became an eminent rustic-genre painter. Roscoe, a Liverpool banker, wrote lives of Lorenzo de Medici and Leo X. The poem was first published in the *Gentleman's Magazine* in 1806. Twenty thousand copies of the illustrated edition sold in a year and follow-up versions proliferated. George III ordered it to be set to music for his daughters.

5 **Anonymous**
REV. ISAAC TAYLOR, *Scenes in England for the Amusement and Instruction of Little Tarry-at-Home Travellers*, London 1821
'Cheviot Shepherds; Bamburgh Castle; Berwick upon Tweed' (showing 'the first cannon ever used in England')
Anonymous engraving: issued in plain and hand-coloured versions.

Taylor produced a large number of Tarry-at-Home books, Bible stories and histories in the same format. His daughters, Anne and Jane, wrote *Original Poems for Infant Minds* (1804), illustrated by his son Isaac.

6 **Thomas Bewick**
Aesop's Fables, With Cuts Designed and Engraved by Thomas and John Bewick and Others, Newcastle upon Tyne 1818
'The Crow and the Pitcher'. Woodcut.

Most of the blocks were cut by pupils from Bewick's drawings.

7 **Heinrich Hoffmann** (1809–1894)
English Struwwelpeter, London *c.* 1900 (n.d.)
'Shock-headed Peter'. Lithograph.

This English version of Struwwelpeter reverted to the simple style of the original edition.

8 **George Cruikshank** (1792–1878)
Comic Alphabet, 'designed, etched, and published by the artist', London 1836

Cruikshank sports his caricaturist origins: 'N' for Nightmare, for example, an image he had previously used several times, with Napoleon and a rogue Lord Mayor of London as the subjects, derives, via Gillray, from Fuseli's *Nightmare*. His other important picture books for children include *John Gilpin* (1828), *Robinson Crusoe* (1831), *The Bee & the Wasp* (1832) and *Fairy Library* (1853–4, 1864).

9 **Heinrich Hoffmann**
Der Struwwelpeter, Frankfurt *c.* 1876 (n.d.)
   '"Ah!" said Mamma, "I knew he'd come
   To naughty little Suck-a-Thumb."'
Wood engraving.

Hoffmann, doctor to a lunatic asylum, wrote and drew Struwwelpeter for his son in 1844. It was designed to be enjoyably scarifying. The illustrations changed considerably after first publication in 1845. Hoffmann did several other, more placid picture books, such as *Der König Nussknacker (The Nutcracker King)* and *Bastian der Faulpelz (Sebastian the Lazybones,* 1854).

10 **Edward Lear** (1817–1864)
A Book of Nonsense, London 1870
'There was an Old Man of the Hague' and 'There was an Old Man who said, "Hush!"'
Wood engravings.

First published in 1846, in black and white. Lear guyed his usual topographic, botanical and zoological drawing.

11 **John Martin** (1789–1854)
Illustrations of the Old and New Testaments by Westall and Martin, London 1835
'The Third Temptation'. Wood engraving.
Martin's Bible imagery had a strong influence on Dante Gabriel and Christina Rossetti and on the Brontës when they were children. Charlotte Brontë adapted this engraving in a drawing of her imaginary city 'Verdopolis' or 'Glasstown'.

12 **Rudolphe Töpffer** (1799–1846)
Voyages et aventures du Docteur Festus, Geneva 1840
Lithograph.
Drawn by the shortsighted Töpffer for his pupils. In this scene from the comic strip story, the doctor appoints vigilantes to keep watch on a flying telescope. Töpffer also published *L'histoire de M. Jabot* (1835) and *L'histoire de M. Crépin* (1837).

13 **Grandville** (pseud. for **Jean-Ignace Gérard,** 1803–1847)
SWIFT, *Travels into Several Remote Nations of the World by Lemuel Gulliver*, Paris 1840
Wood engraving.

14 **Theodor Hosemann** (1807–1875)
'TANTE AMIADA', *Eine Häschen und eine Kätzchen Geschichte*, Berlin 1872

15 **John Leech** (1817–1864)
GILBERT À BECKETT, *Comic History of England*, London 1847
'The landing of Julius Caesar'. Coloured etching.
Leech and à Beckett also collaborated on a *Comic Latin Grammar*. Here Leech mocks both the grand Maclise school of history painting, and textbook truisms. Cruikshank taught him to etch.

16 **James E. Doyle** (1822–1892)
A Chronicle of England, London 1864
'The murder of the Duke of Suffolk, 1450'. Colour printing by Edmund Evans.
Elder brother of Richard Doyle and heraldic expert. The illustrations to his sumptuously produced history are neat vignettes surrounded by dry text.

17 **Richard Doyle** (1824–1883)
W. ALLINGHAM, *In Fairyland*, London 1870
'The Elf-King asleep'. Wood engraving: colour printing by Edmund Evans.
Richard Doyle worked for *Punch* in its early years and illustrated *The Enchanted Doll* (1849) by the editor, Mark Lemon. *In Fairyland*, Doyle's masterpiece, was published at the height of the Victorian fairy cult.

18 **George Cruikshank**
GIAMBATTISTA BASILE, *The Pentamerone*, London 1848
'Peruonto riding on the faggot past the palace' and 'Vardiello chasing the cat'. Etching.

Basile, a mercenary, made his collection of Neapolitan folk tales in the 1630s. Cruikshank's ornate mature style was even further developed in his *Fairy Library*.

19 **William Makepeace Thackeray** (1811–1863)
The Rose and the Ring, London 1855
'Bulbo led away (weeping) to execution'. Wood engraving.
Thackeray described it as 'a fireside pantomime'. His style reflects Cruikshank's Regency caricatures.

20 **Wilhelm Busch** (1832–1908)
Max und Moritz, Munich 1865
'*Schnupdiwup! da wird nach oben
Schon ein Huhn heraufgehoben*'
Wood engraving.
Busch developed his line in comic horror stories in the *Münchener Bilderbogen* and perfected a mime, or shadowplay, narrative form. His first book, *Die Bilderpossen* (*Pranks in Pictures*) was published in 1864.

21 **Richard Doyle**
J. RUSKIN, *The King of the Golden River*, London 1851
'South-West Wind, Esq., knocking at the Black Brothers' door'. Wood engraving.
Ruskin originally wrote the story in 1841 for a child, Effie Gray, to whom he was later married for a short time.

22 **Gustave Doré** (1832–1883)
M. DE CERVANTES, *History of Don Quixote*, London and Paris 1863
'The sail hurled away both knight and horse along with it'. Wood engraving.
Doré began as a caricaturist and ended as a painter of vast biblical scenes; at mid-career, in *Don Quixote*, his concerns are nicely balanced. He also illustrated *Perrault's Fairy Tales* (1867) and *The Adventures of Baron Munchhausen* (1866).

23 **Walter Crane** (1845–1915)
The Frog Prince, engraved and printed by Edmund Evans, London 1874
'The Princess shares her dinner with the frog'. Wood engraving.
A dominant figure in the Arts and Crafts Movement from 1885, Crane worked for a while with William Morris, but his most important collaboration was with the printer Edmund Evans. Evans printed many Crane 'toy books': fairy stories, alphabets and nursery rhymes, notably *The Baby's Opera* (1877).

24 **Randolph Caldecott** (1846–1886)
Sing a Song for Sixpence, engraved and printed by Edmund Evans, London 1880
Caldecott learnt to tint his drawings in colour combinations that would suit his printer. His illustrations to Cowper's *Diverting History of John Gilpin* (1878) are more typical of his bustling style.

25 Kate Greenaway (1846–1901)
Mother Goose, engraved and printed by Edmund
Evans, London 1881
'Hark! hark! the dogs bark'
Kate Greenaway, the daughter of an engraver,
made her name with *Under the Window* (1878).
Twenty thousand copies were sold immediately and
a Greenaway craze began, stimulated further by
Mother Goose (1881) and *Marigold Garden* (1885).

26 Moritz von Schwind (1804–1871)
'Puss in Boots', in the *Münchener Bilderbogen*, Munich
1850
Broadsheets such as this, accommodating narrative
in picture form, contained some of the most vigorous
nineteenth-century German illustration.

27 John Tenniel (1820–1914)
LEWIS CARROLL, *Alice's Adventures in Wonderland*,
London 1865
'The Mad Hatter's Tea Party'

28 LEWIS CARROLL, *Alice Through the Looking Glass*,
London 1871
'Alice and the White Queen'
Tenniel trained as a painter before turning to
political caricature for *Punch*, succeeding Leech in
1864. Carroll supervised every detail of his
illustrations for the *Alice* books. 'Lewis Carroll is
impossible,' Tenniel said.

29 Walter Crane
Beauty and the Beast, London 1875
'There she found poor Beast stretched out, quite
senseless'
Coloured wood engraving by Edmund Evans.

30 M. Boutet de Monvel (1850–1913)
J. PLON, *Jeanne d'Arc*, Paris 1896
Lithograph.
Boutet de Monvel used lithography with great
subtlety and restraint. He also illustrated Anatole
France's *Nos enfants* and *Filles et garçons*.

31 Francis Bedford (1864–1950)
E. V. LUCAS, *The Book of Shops*, London 1899
'The village store'
Bedford, an architect turned illustrator, specialized
in Garden Suburb idylls: a blend of Crane and de
Monvel. He also illustrated *Old English Fairy Tales* (1895).

32 A. B. Frost (1851–1928)
JOEL CHANDLER HARRIS, *Uncle Remus: His Songs and
His Sayings*, New York 1895
Like his friend Howard Pyle, A. B. Frost relied on
photo process for reproduction. This enabled him to
draw freely without worry about the transfer of fine
lines, by hand, on to the block. He also illustrated
Tom Sawyer.

33 Maxfield Parrish (1870–1966)
KENNETH GRAHAME, *The Golden Age*, London and
New York 1899
'It was easy . . .'
Parrish once described himself as 'a mechanic who
paints'. He became famed for his magazine-cover
girls, musing beside blue mountains. Kaiser Wilhelm
II ordered twelve copies of *The Golden Age*. A sequel,
Dream Days (1900–1) was also illustrated by
Parrish, as was L. Frank Baum's *Mother Goose in Prose*
(1897).

34 Ernest Griset (1844–1907)
Bo-Peep: A Treasury for the Little Ones, London *c.* 1880
(n.d.)
'The return home'
Griset was born in France but worked in London for
the Dalziel brothers and for *Punch*. He illustrated
Robinson Crusoe (1869), *Aesop's Fables* (1869, 1893)
and did black-comic designs for James Breenwood's
The Hatchet Throwers (1866) and *Legends of Savage Life*
(1867).

35 Howard Pyle (1853–1911)
The Merry Adventures of Robin Hood, New York 1883
'Little John in ye guise of a friar stops three lasses'
Pyle's own stories and devilled-medieval
illustrations, e.g. *Otto of the Silver Hand* (1888) and
four volumes of Arthurian romances (1903–10), were
acclaimed for their spirit. Pyle believed that text and
illustration should 'round the circle instead of
advancing in parallel lines'.

36 Carl Larsson (1853–1919)
Ett Hem, Stockholm 1904.
'Mammas och småflickornas rum'. Lithograph.
Essentially an idealized family album.

37 Florence K. Upton (1873–1922)
BERTHA UPTON, *The Adventures of Two Dutch Dolls*,
London 1895
   'And now the Ball is at its height,
   A madly whirling throng'
Lithograph.
Florence Upton (daughter of Bertha) invented the
name 'Golliwog'. Picture books about dolls
developed alongside the toy industry from the 1870s.

38 Ivan A. Bilibin (1876–1942?)
PUSHKIN, *Skazka ob Ivané-Tsaréviche, zhár-ptitse io serom
vólke* (*The Story of Ivan the Crown Prince, the Firebird and
the Grey Wolf*), St Petersburg 1899. Lithograph.
Bilibin's illustrations were equivalent in impact to
the pre-war Russian ballet: rich shadows, gilded
highlights and sudden outbursts of colour.

39 W. Heath Robinson (1869–1944)
The Adventures of Uncle Lubin, London 1902
'Uncle Lubin was able to start on his voyage'

Heath Robinson began as an all-purpose illustrator (like his father and brothers). Eventually his drawings of intricate contraptions (anticipated here) led him away from book illustration proper. 'Heath Robinson' became an adjective describing dotty, makeshift mechanisms.

40 **John Hassall** (1868–1948)
DANIEL DEFOE, *The Adventures of Robinson Crusoe*, London, Glasgow and Bombay *c.* 1900 (n.d.)
'Crusoe and his pets at meal times'
John Hassall, a prolific poster and advertising artist, designed many of the best pictorial covers for Nelson and Blackie children's books *c.* 1890–1920. His standard gauge linework suited the cheap, spongy paper of reward books and annuals.

41 **Lyonel Feininger** (1871–1956)
The Kin-der-Kids Relief-Expedition, Chicago Sunday Tribune (comic section), 1 July 1906
Born in New York, Feininger worked for German magazines such as *Humoristische Blätter* and the *Berliner Blätter*. He developed the 'Kin-der-Kids' as a cartoon gang to rival the 'Yellow Kid', the 'Katzenjammer Kids' of Rudolph Dirks and Winsor McCay's 'Little Nemo'. He went on to make his artistic reputation with a highly refined expresso-cubism.

42 **W. Heath Robinson**
Grant Richard's Children's Annual, edited by R. W. H. Crossland, London 1904
'The Battle'
The best English children's annual of the early 1900s.

43 **Max Dasio** (1865–1954)
Hoffmann Fibel für den vereinigten Sprach=, Schreib= und Leseunterricht, Munich *c.* 1900 (n.d.)
An elegant German school primer. Max Dasio was a professor at the Munich art school.

44 **Willy Pogany** (b. 1882)
GRACE BARTRUSE, *The Children in Japan*, New York 1915
'They came at length to Mount Fuji'
Born in Hungary, Willy Pogany went to America in 1915 and worked as an art director in Hollywood.

45 **Winsor McCay** (1871–1934)
Little Nemo in Slumberland, New York Herald, December 1908
McCay's comic-strip hero wanders every night in his dreams. 'Critics say my knowledge of perspective makes my drawings look snappy,' said McCay.

46 **Leslie Brooke** (1862–1940)
Johnny Crow's Party, London 1907
'*But the Giraffe*
Was inclined to laugh'

Sequel to *Johnny Crow's Garden* (1903) and followed by *Johnny Crow's New Garden* (1935). A last flowering of the Crane-Caldecott toybook mode.

47 **N. C. Wyeth** (1882–1945)
S. LANIER, *The Boy's King Arthur*, New York and London 1920
'Sir Mador's spear brake all to pieces but the other's spear held'

48 **Arthur Rackham** (1867–1939)
J. M. BARRIE, *Peter Pan in Kensington Gardens*, London 1906
'The Kensington Gardens are in London, where the King lives'
The first luxury gift-book Rackham illustrated. His style depended on washed-out tones and violent contrasts of the gnarled and the ethereal.

49 **N. C. Wyeth**
J. FENIMORE COOPER, *The Last of the Mohicans*, New York and London 1920
'The Battle at Glens Falls'
N. C. Wyeth's brand of picturesque realism (see also *Treasure Island*, 1911) was continued by his son Andrew Wyeth.

50 **Beatrix Potter** (1866–1943)
The Tale of Benjamin Bunny, London 1904
'Benjamin, on the contrary, was perfectly at home, and ate a lettuce leaf'
Beatrix Potter's first book, *The Tale of Peter Rabbit*, published privately in 1901, began as a letter to a little boy. *The Tailor of Gloucester* (1902), *The Tale of Squirrel Nutkin* (1903), *The Tale of Benjamin Bunny* and *The Tale of Two Bad Mice* (1904) followed. In 1905 she bought Hill Top Farm in the Lake District and this inspired some of her best books: *The Pie and the Patty Pan* (1905), *Tom Kitten* (1906), *Jemima Puddleduck* (1907), *The Roly-Poly Pudding* (1908), *Ginger and Pickles* (1909) and *Pigling Bland* (1913). After her marriage in 1913 she became a sheep farmer with little time for books.

51 **John R. Neill**
L. FRANK BAUM, *The Marvellous Land of Oz*, London and New York 1904
'The stranger removed his hat with a flourish'
The Wizard of Oz, the first of L. Frank Baum's fourteen Oz books, was published in 1899; but they were hardly known outside the U.S.A. until Judy Garland starred as Dorothy in 1939.

52 **Arthur Rackham**
The Allies Fairy Book, London and Philadelphia 1916
'At the dead time of the night in came the Welsh giant'

53 Ogden's 'Guinea Gold' cigarette cards. Photographs.

'Mabel Roma', from a series of four thousand actresses and personalities which began in 1894.
'Lieut.-Gen. Baden Powell', from a series on Boy Scouts, 1911.
'Statue to Mr Kruger in Pretoria', a Boer War series, 1900.

54 Trade cards, given away with coffee, French, *c.* 1910
A series of over eighty cards showing the wonders of electricity.

55 Trade stamps, German, *c.* 1914
Thousands of different designs were produced, either advertising the goods directly (e.g. Liebig's Fleisch Extract) or in series of fairy tales, beauty spots, famous buildings, sports, etc.

56 **Kay Nielsen** (1886–1957)
East of the Sun, West of the Moon, London 1914
'The Lad in Battle'
Kay Nielsen, born in Copenhagen, spent his working life in England and the United States. Besides illustrating and painting murals he acted, directed and designed stage sets.

57 **Edmund Dulac** (1882–1953)
Stories from Hans Andersen, London 1912
'I have hardly closed my eyes all night'
Born in Toulouse, Dulac settled in England and by 1912 was established with Rackham as a dominant luxury-book illustrator. He illustrated *Treasure Island* in 1927, with his usual Persian-miniature tinge. He also designed the George VI Coronation stamp in 1937, and made models of George Moore in wax.

58 *Edmund Dulac's Fairy Book*, London 1915
'The Palace of the Dragon King'

59 **Kay Nielsen**
Hansel and Gretel and other stories by the Brothers Grimm, London 1925

60 **Benjamin Rabier** (1869–?)
Scènes de la vie privée des animaux, Paris *c.* 1910 (n.d.)
'Singulier personnage, ou le jars endimanché'
Rabier's series of picture books of comic animals began in the 1880s.

61 **K. F. von Freyhold** (1878–1944)
CHRISTIAN MORGENSTERN, *Hasenbuch*, Berlin 1920
'Das Osterhaus ist eben fertig'
An outstanding picture book from the German publishing revival after the First World War. In 1904, together with Karl Hofer and Kreidolf, Freyhold illustrated a collection of poems, *Buntscheck*.

62 **André Hellé** (1871–?)
Fables de La Fontaine, Nancy 1922
'Le lion abattu par l'homme'

Hellé's designs were drawn to resemble woodcuts and were coloured by the pochoir (hand-stencilling) method. His first book was *Noah's Ark* (1914). He also designed toys and ballets.

63 **O. Stáfl**
V. TILLE, *Little Tom*, Prague 1922
'Little Tom found himself in a clock with a cuckoo and thought he was in an enchanted castle . . . he saw about him, in every direction, wheels, levers, teeth and cylinders. Everything was moving and turning around'

64 **Hugh Lofting** (1886–1947)
The Story of Doctor Dolittle, New York 1920
'An enormous footprint'
Dr Lofting's stories and guileless illustrations stemmed from his letter from the Western Front to his children. Born in England, he worked for most of his life in America, where *The Story of Doctor Dolittle* was first published.

65 **Marcel de Vinck**
Lord Pington découvre l'Amérique, Paris *c.* 1925 (n.d.)
'A great feast in which the whole tribe took part'

66 **Claud Lovat Fraser** (1890–1921)
Nursery Rhymes, London 1922
'Patty-cake, patty-cake'
Like André Hellé, Lovat Fraser revived chapbook mannerisms. He designed stage sets and toys (*A Book of Simple Toys*, 1917) in much the same quasi-naïve style.

67 **Edy Legrand** (*b.* 1901)
Macao et Cosmage, Paris 1919
Pochoir process.
Legrand produced this celebration of jazz modernity when he was eighteen. In *Voyages et glorieuses découvertes des grands navigateurs et explorateurs français* (1921), he consolidated his panache and later settled into a more prosaic, all-purpose vein (*Petite histoire de La Fayette* and *Bolivar* (1929)).

68 **Anonymous**
Outdoor Fun – Games Everyone Can Play, New York 1935
'Chicken market'. Lithograph.

69 **Anonymous**
'Les enfants imprudents!' Trade card, Belgian, *c.* 1925
One of a series on road safety issued by a cheese firm.

70 **Attilio Mussino** (1878–?)
COLLODI, *Le avventure di Pinocchio*, Florence 1924
Carlo Lorenzini's (Collodi's) book first appeared *c.* 1883. Mussino's illustrations were definitive until Disney rejigged Pinocchio Tyrolean-style in 1940.

71 Walter Trier (1890–1951)
Erich Kästner, *Arthur mit dem langen Arm*, Berlin 1931

> '*Trude krähte wie ein Sänger*
> *Arthurs Arm ward lang und länger*'

Trier started out as a cartoonist for *Simplicissimus*. He illustrated Kästner's *Emil and the Detectives* (1929). In 1936 he left Germany for England, where he worked on *Lilliput* until 1946, and became particularly good at doing Goering.

72 Jodel (J. de Lalande,
?–1940)
Napoléon, Paris *c.* 1925 (n.d.)
'Le couronnement'. Pochoir process.

Tolmer, who printed *Napoléon*, also published Legrand's *Voyages et glorieuses découvertes des grands navigateurs et explorateurs français*, *Bolivar* and *La Fayette*.

73 Feodor Rojankovsky (*b.* 1891)
Daniel Boone, Paris, New York and London 1931
'In 1774 War was declared on the Indian Tribes'. Lithograph.

This first book by Rojankovsky, a White Russian émigré living in Paris, was published simultaneously in Paris, New York and London. Rojankovsky went on to illustrate the Père Castor albums.

74 Leslie Carr
By Road, Rail, Air and Sea, London *c.* 1930 (n.d.)
'At the petrol station'

75 William Nicholson (1872–1949)
The Pirate Twins, London 1929
'What "S" Stands for'. Lithograph.

When young, Nicholson and James Pryde, calling themselves the Beggarstaff brothers, produced posters. Later Nicholson's *Alphabet* and *London Types* (both published 1898) established a new look in picture books. His first children's book, *Velveteen Rabbit*, was published in 1922, followed by *Clever Bill* in 1926.

76 Kurt Schwitters (1887–1948)
Kate Steinitz (?–1975)
Theo van Doesburg (1883–1931)
Die Scheuche Märchen, Hanover 1925

> '*Da forschte*
> *Sich der Hut-Schapo*'

Not so much a children's book as a New Typographic Dada plaything. Schwitters also made *Die Märchen vom Paradies* in 1924.

77 Emmanuel Sougez
Alphabet, Paris 1932
'T TABLE'. Photograph.

78 Friedrich Boer (*b.* 1904)
Klaus der Herr der Eisenbahnen, Berlin 1933
'On the platform'

Friedrich Boer produced two mixed media books in the early 1930s (this one about a boy and a railway, the other about three boys exploring a town), using a photo-collage technique together with red and half-tone retouchings.

79 Marianne Scheel (*b.* 1902)
Krischan der Bauernjunge, Berlin 1934
'October'

The story of a year in a farm boy's life. Marianne Scheel's books, concerned primarily with nature and the countryside, include *Die Jahreszeiten* (1935) and *Die Geschichte von der Wiese* (1945).

80 Anonymous
Koshkin Dom, Moscow 1937

One of a series of tiny books, printed in five colours. 'We want books that say what they have to say in an enjoyable manner so that children develop a sense of humour,' wrote Maxim Gorky as a Party spokesman in 1933.

81 Nathalie Parain
Crayons et ciseaux, Paris *c.* 1932 (n.d.)
'L'orage'

Père Castor, a Parisian bookseller, produced over two hundred and fifty work books, story books, games and calendars. Nathalie Parain and Rojankovsky were responsible for many of the best. Nathalie Parain also designed a brilliant series of cutout albums (e.g. *Je découpe*) and illustrated some of Marcel Aymé's *Les contes du chat perché* in fine nursery-Léger style.

82 Ernest Shepard (1879–1976)
Kenneth Grahame, *The Wind in the Willows*, London 1931
'Mole and Rat load the picnic'

Ernest Shepard's characterizations of Mole, Rat and Toad established the look of the story (first published in 1908) for the first time. He did the same for A. A. Milne's *Winnie-the-Pooh* (1926).

83 Vladimir Lebedev (*b.* 1891)
S. Marshak, *Pudel*, Leningrad 1934

Printed in black and terracotta on cheap blue paper. A political poster artist, Lebedev also illustrated children's books during the thirties.

84 Feodor Rojankovsky
Y. Lacote, *Calendrier des enfants*, Paris 1936
'Février'

> '*Glace, dégel, verglas,*
> *n'empêchent pas*
> *mardi gras*
> *de faire sauter la crêpe*
> *et dorer le beignet*'

Rojankovsky also illustrated a series about wild animals for Père Castor, including *Scaf* (a seal,

1934), *Panache* (a squirrel, 1934) and *Plouf* (a wild duck, 1935). In 1941 he moved to America.

85 **Wanda Gág** (1893–1946)
Millions of Cats, New York 1928
'And they began to quarrel'
> '*Cats here, cats there,*
> *Cats and kittens everywhere,*
> *Hundreds of cats,*
> *Thousands of cats,*
> *Millions and billions and trillions of cats*'

Wanda Gág's best work is in black and white, as here and in *Tales from Grimm* (1936).

86 **Vladimir Konashevich**
Kornei Chukovsky, *Tarakanischche (The Cockroach)*, Leningrad 1935
Colour lithograph.

87 **Garcin Jo**
L'auto, a Petit Mécano album, Paris 1930

88 **Elsa Moeschlin** (1879–1950)
Vrenelis Skizzenbuch, Oldenburg 1933
'Sonntagsausflug'

89 **Hergé (Georges Rémi,** *b.* 1907)
Tintin: Les sept boules de cristal, Tournai and Paris *c.* 1938
The adventures of the knickerbockered cub reporter and his dog Snowy began in 1929 with *Tintin au pays des Soviets* and have continued, apart from a wartime break, for thirty-five years.

90 **Pierre Noury** (*b.* 1894)
Le Prince Toto Che, Paris 1933. Lithograph.

91 **Boris Artzybasheff** (*b.* 1899)
Seven Simeons: A Russian Tale, New York 1937
'King Douda welcomes Helena to his kingdom'
A deft, stripped-down version of Bilibin material in neon-coloured line, by a Russian emigré working in New York. Artzybasheff has since designed over two hundred covers for *Time* magazine.

92 **Mary Tourtel** (*d.* 1935)
Rupert: Three Stories of the Little Bear's Adventures, London *c.* 1930
'Rupert and the magician's umbrella'
First appeared in 1920 as a cartoon, *The Adventures of a Little Lost Bear*, in the *Daily Express*, and was reissued in annual form. Since Mary Tourtel's death in 1935, the series has been continued by A. E. Bestall.

93 **Jan Lewitt** (*b.* 1907) and **George Him** (*b.* 1900)
Julian Tuwin, *Locomotywa*, Warsaw 1938
The Lewitt-Him partnership began in 1933 and lasted for twenty years. They moved to London in 1938, where *Country Life* published their *Footballers' Revolt* in the same deft, streamlined idiom.

94 **Jean de Brunhoff** (1899–1937)
Histoire de Babar le petit éléphant, Paris 1931
'Très content de ses achats et satisfait . . .'
Lithograph.
Jean de Brunhoff wrote six Babar books, the first being *Histoire de Babar le petit éléphant* (1931). The series has been continued and spun out by his son, Laurent de Brunhoff.

95 **Harold Jones** (*b.* 1904)
Walter de la Mare, *This Year: Next Year*, London 1937
'Esmeralda'. Lithograph.
Harold Jones drew the lithographs and wrote his own poems for *This Year: Next Year*. These were taken over by de la Mare and rewritten.

96 **Edward Ardizzone** (*b.* 1900)
Little Tim and the Brave Sea Captain, Oxford 1936
'When it was wet Tim would visit Captain McFee, who would tell him about his voyages and sometimes give him a sip of his grog, which made Tim want to be a sailor more than ever'
Initially Ardizzone's 'Little Tim' books, of which *Little Tim and the Brave Sea Captain* is the first, were lithographed and folio size: but during the war economies were made, the handwritten scripts were replaced by letterpress and the size reduced. Eventually Ardizzone made fresh illustrations.

97 **Ernst Rüegg** (1883–1948)
Das Jahr des Bauern, Zürich 1941
'Then the first rainbow appears, and the sun shines again on the rain-drenched fields'
The *Atlantis Kinderbücher* series, started in Zurich in 1935, was mainly concerned with outdoor topics: food, mountain climbing, farming and general well-being.

98 **Clarke Hutton** (*b.* 1898)
Noel Streatfeild, *Harlequinade*, London 1943
'Serge was upside down. His head looked through his hands at the old man'
Clarke Hutton wrote and illustrated a series of Picture Histories of Britain, France, Canada, Russia, etc.

99 **Virginia Lee Burton** (1909–68)
The Little House, Boston 1942
'One day the Little House was surprised to see a horseless carriage coming down the winding country road'
Virginia Lee Burton wrote and illustrated *Calico the Wonder Horse* (1939) and *Mike Mulligan and his Steam Shovel* (1939) in the same vigorous manner.

100 Leslie Wood

Diana Ross, *The Little Red Engine Goes to Market*, London 1945
Lithograph.

The continuation of a series begun by Lewitt-Him in 1942 with *The Little Red Engine Gets a Name* and foreshadowed in their *Locomotywa* (1938).

101 Margaret and Alexander Potter

A History of the Countryside, London 1943
'Ribbon development'. Lithograph.

Puffin Picture Books, of which this was one, were started in 1940 following on from Russian paperbacks and the Père Castor albums. With a few exceptions (such as *Orlando's Evening Out*) the books, edited by Noel Carrington, dealt with factual subject matter. The series eventually amounted to well over a hundred titles and lasted until the mid 1960s.

Margaret and Alexander Potter also did *The Building of London* (1945) for Puffin, and *Houses* (1948) and *Interiors* (1957), which were published by John Murray.

102 Kathleen Hale (*b.* 1898)

Orlando's Evening Out, London 1941
'The Circus had begun'

'I believe in basing fantasy on reality,' writes Kathleen Hale. Beginning with *Orlando and the Marmalade Cat* (1937), the early titles in the Orlando series first appeared folio-size and were intended as an English equivalent to Babar. *Orlando's Evening Out* was published as a paperback by Puffin/Harlequin. Other titles include *Orlando's Home Life* (1942) and *Orlando: His Silver Wedding* (1944).

103 Edward Burra (*b.* 1905)

Mark Twain, *Huckleberry Finn*, London 1947
'The segars was prime. We laid off all the afternoon in the woods talking, and me reading the books, and having a general good time'

As a painter, Burra's speciality is sinister characters and shady transactions in fancy locales. *Huckleberry Finn*, one of the few books he has illustrated, suited his devices.

104 C. Walter Hodges (*b.* 1909)

Columbus Sails, London 1939

Walter Hodges, who also wrote the story of *Columbus Sails*, has specialized in robust, slightly cinematic historical reconstruction.

105 Brian Robb (*b.* 1913)

The Adventures of the Celebrated Baron Munchhausen, London 1947

'The ship struck with amazing force against (as we supposed) a rock'.

106 John Minton (1917–1957)

R. L. Stevenson, *Treasure Island*, London 1947
'Long John Silver'

From the same series (Camden Classics) as Burra's *Huckleberry Finn*.

107 Mervyn Peake (1911–1968)

R. L. Stevenson, *Treasure Island*, London 1949
'The storming of the stockade'

Mervyn Peake was a painter turned illustrator and writer (*Gormenghast*, 1950 and *Titus Groan*, 1959). His books for children include *Captain Slaughterboard Drops Anchor* (1939) and a book of nursery rhymes, *Ride a Cock Horse* (1940).

108 Maurice Sendak (*b.* 1928)

In the Night Kitchen
London, New York 1971

Acknowledgments

For loans, advice and information the author wishes to thank: Edward Ardizzone, Noel Carrington, Susan Collier, Kathleen Hale, Ilse, Charlotte and Sophie Herxheimer, Harold Jones, Peggy Kilbourn, Nicholas Logsdail, Brian Mills, Margaret and Alexander Potter, Kaye Webb and Ellery Yale Wood. Special thanks are due to Vicki Feaver for her invaluable help at every stage.

Illustrations reprinted by permission of the following:
Atlantis Verlag AG, Zürich 97. Atrium Verlag AG, Zürich 71. G. Bell & Sons, London 104. Blackie and Son Ltd, Glasgow 40, 74. The Bodley Head, London 33. Jonathan Cape Ltd, London 65. Bruno Cassirer, Oxford 61. Casterman, Tournai Art © 89. Chatto & Windus Ltd, London 98. *Chicago Tribune* 41. Coward, McCann & Geoghegan, Inc., New York 84 (copyright 1928 by Coward-McCann, Inc., renewed). Curtis Brown Ltd, London 85 (line illustrations by Ernest H. Shepard copyright under the Berne Convention; copyright in USA Charles Scribner's Sons; renewal copyright © 1961 Ernest H. Shepard). Paul Elek Archives, London 103, 106. Faber and Faber Ltd, London 99, 100. Flammarion et Cie, Paris 81, 83, 90. Gallimard, Paris 67. Hachette, Paris 64, 87, 94. William Heinemann Ltd, London 52. Hodder & Stoughton Children's Books, Leicester 56, 57, 58, 59. Houghton Mifflin Company, Boston, Mass. 99. Christopher Lofting 65. Methuen & Co. Ltd, London 94. Minerva Press Ltd, London 39. Oxford University Press, London 96. Mrs Maeve Peake 107. Penguin Books Ltd, Harmondsworth 101 © Margaret and Alexander Potter, 1940), 102 © Kathleen Hale, 1941). Prentice-Hall, Inc., Englewood Cliffs, NJ 32. Charles Scribner's Sons, New York 47 (illustration copyright 1917 Charles Scribner's Sons; renewal copyright 1945 N. C. Wyeth), 48 (illustration copyright 1919 Charles Scribner's Sons; renewal copyright 1947 Carolyn B. Wyeth), 85 illustration copyright 1933 Charles Scribner's Sons). Tolmer et Fils, Paris 72. Viking Penguin, Inc., New York 91 (copyright 1937, copyright © renewed 1965 by Boris Artzybasheff). Frederick Warne & Co., Ltd, London 46, 50.